WILD SOUTH CAROLINA

WILD

SOUTH CAROLINA

A Field Guide to Parks,
Preserves and Special Places

LIESEL & SUSAN HAMILTON
PHOTOS BY TORI STEYNE

First printing, October 2016

Editor: Betsy Teter
Project assistant: Erin Mathers
Cover and interior design: Brandy Lindsey & The Graphics House
Proofreaders: Mary-Peyton Crook, Beverly Knight, Tim Marsh, and Jan Scalisi
Printed in Korea by Four Colour Print Group, Louisville, Kentucky

All photos by Tori Steyne, Liesel Hamilton (pages 16, 17, 19, 61, 63, 79, 80, 97), Susan Hamilton (pages 25, 27, 87, 109, 114), and Frank W. Baker (page 121).

Library of Congress Cataloging-in-Publication Data available online at loc.gov

186 West Main Street
Spartanburg, SC 29306
hubcity.org

CONTENTS

INTRODUCTION BY LIESEL HAMILTON

Our family has called Columbia, South Carolina, home for more than two decades, and during that time, we have spent countless hours hiking, camping, and enjoying what the state has to offer. But, like many residents, we had missed many lesser-known destinations. Thanks to participating in some naturalist classes, this mother/daughter team discovered a slew of new and extraordinary destinations. We made a pact to go on a journey—just us in the great outdoors—visiting as many state parks, wildlife refuges, historic sites, heritage preserves, county parks, and other natural areas as we possibly could.

And so we began. On our trip to Caw Caw Interpretive Center near Charleston, we experienced an astonishing rainbow of colors glistening atop swampy water—a miraculous phenomenon that occurs in southern swamps on sunny winter days. At Hunting Island and Lighthouse Inlet Heritage Preserve, we observed strong, silent lighthouses absorbing the pounding South Carolina surf. At Lewis Ocean Bay Heritage Preserve we saw Venus flytraps—a species that can only survive in the Carolinas—snapping their green jaws closed amidst delicate ferns, suffocating wandering beetles that drifted too close to their sticky pink centers. In the fields of Stevens Creek Heritage Preserve near McCormick we witnessed hundreds of wildflowers blooming triumphantly—trilliums, shooting stars, and orchids. And in the riverbed at Landsford Canal near Lancaster we beheld thousands of white spider lilies flourishing in a cloud of white.

South Carolina has 73 heritage preserves, 47 state parks, five state forests, two national forests, and one national park, as well as countless other public parks, beaches, and open areas. After exploring all corners of our state, we created a tight list of 38 places that all South Carolinians should make a point to see, reflecting the natural diversity within the Palmetto State. Each location has a variety of activities or contains something truly unique that you would be hard-pressed to find elsewhere.

No matter where you live in South Carolina, there is likely a state park within 30 minutes of your home. Our state park system was conceived in 1933 during the Great Depression and was created through the work of the Civilian Conservation Corps (CCC), which developed 16 state parks from the mountains to the coastline. Cheraw was the first state park, and it is still one of our favorites with its well-maintained longleaf pine forest and slow-moving river where blue flag irises and yellow pitcher plants make for one of the most incredible flower displays in the state. In each CCC location, facilities were constructed using local materials, so all of these sites contain unique, historical buildings. These parks have facilities made of longleaf pines, rare coquina stone, granite, and many other materials that reflect the diversity of our state's resources.

There are 31 other state parks and state historic sites that are equally as interesting, acquired in later years as property and financing became available. One of the best ways to see all the park system has to offer is to purchase a statewide park pass, available at any park location and good for an entire carload of visitors. Without the pass, the parks charge a nominal admittance fee that varies depending on location and infrastructure, generally beginning at about $2 per person for each visit. With camping, picnic facilities, maintained hiking trails, restrooms, and other amenities, the parks are a great place to enjoy outdoor adventures.

Often overlooked are the large number of heritage preserves. The Heritage Trust program was founded in 1976 specifically to conserve natural features and resources that were quickly vanishing from the landscape. South Carolina was the first state in the nation to create this program, which has since been duplicated in other states. Again, we've whittled these sites down to create a less overwhelming list; generally we have included sites that are interesting for more than one plant, animal, or geological formation. Heritage preserves are free, but they are not particularly well-maintained. None have restroom facilities. The Department of Natural Resources website (dnr.sc.gov) provides directions to each preserve, often indicated by a simple sign and gravel parking lot. We found it useful to take smartphone pictures of posted maps, if available, at the entrance.

The U.S. Fish and Wildlife Service

Liesel, left, and Susan Hamilton

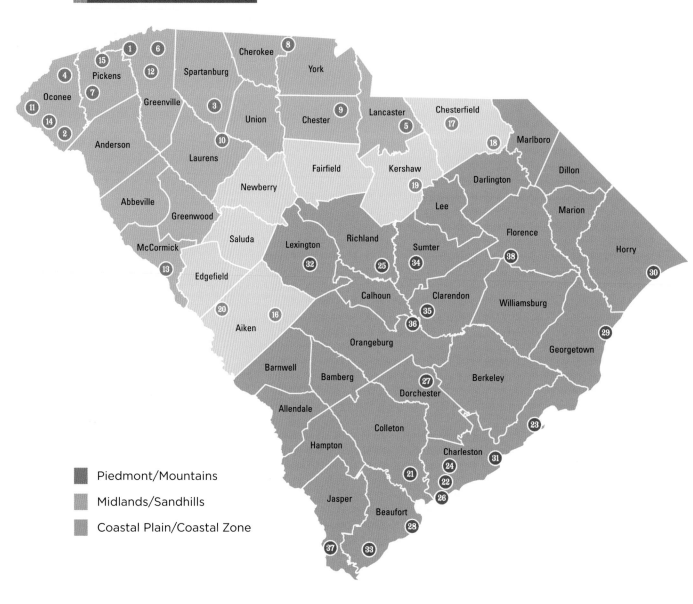

South Carolina Counties

Cherokee · Spartanburg · York · Pickens · Greenville · Union · Chester · Lancaster · Chesterfield · Marlboro · Oconee · Anderson · Laurens · Fairfield · Kershaw · Darlington · Dillon · Abbeville · Newberry · Marion · Greenwood · Saluda · Lexington · Richland · Sumter · Florence · Horry · McCormick · Edgefield · Calhoun · Clarendon · Williamsburg · Lee · Aiken · Orangeburg · Georgetown · Barnwell · Bamberg · Dorchester · Berkeley · Allendale · Colleton · Charleston · Hampton · Jasper · Beaufort

Piedmont/Mountains
Midlands/Sandhills
Coastal Plain/Coastal Zone

Activities Legend

 Hiking
 Camping
 Fishing
 Boating/Paddling
 Swimming
 Bird-Watching
 Equestrian Activities
 Photography
 Exploring History
 Lodging
 Biking

Piedmont/Mountains

1. Caesars Head State Park
2. Chau Ram County Park
3. Croft State Park
4. Devils Fork State Park
5. Forty Acre Rock Heritage Preserve
6. Jones Gap State Park
7. Keowee Toxaway State Park
8. Kings Mountain State Park
9. Landsford Canal State Park
10. Musgrove Mill State Historic Site
11. Oconee State Park/Oconee Station Historic Site
12. Paris Mountain State Park
13. Stevens Creek Heritage Preserve
14. Stumphouse Mountain HP/Yellow Branch Falls
15. Table Rock State Park

Midlands/Sandhills

16. Aiken State Park
17. Carolina Sandhills National Wildlife Refuge
18. Cheraw State Park
19. Goodale State Park
20. Hitchcock Woods

Coastal Plain/Coastal Zone

21. Bear Island and Donnelley Wildlife Management Areas
22. Botany Bay Plantation Heritage Preserve
23. Bulls Island
24. Caw Caw Interpretive Center
25. Congaree National Park
26. Edisto Beach State Park
27. Francis Beidler Forest
28. Hunting Island State Park
29. Huntington Beach State Park
30. Lewis Ocean Bay Heritage Preserve
31. Lighthouse Inlet Heritage Preserve
32. Peachtree Rock Heritage Preserve
33. Pinckney Island National Wildlife Refuge
34. Poinsett State Park
35. Santee National Wildlife Refuge
36. Santee State Park
37. Savannah National Wildlife Refuge
38. Woods Bay State Park

maintains eight national wildlife refuges. The refuges offer a variety of activities, from hiking and birdwatching to hunting and fishing. Most of these locations have restroom facilities, although they are few and far between, and most have staffed visitors' centers. Because these refuges are so large, you might want to begin with a driving tour in order to get an overview of the site before deciding on a specific trail. Wildlife refuges also are free, but different sections may be open only seasonally and during specific hours. It is a good idea to check the U.S. Fish and Wildlife Service website for details about each location. Refuges that cater to endangered or migrating birds are sometimes closed during nesting periods, and areas may be closed during hunting seasons as well.

State and national forests are generally less visited than other natural areas, and they are often noted for their large areas of natural landscape with hiking and camping facilities.

We also have included a few other natural sites we feel are particularly noteworthy: Francis Beidler Forest is managed by the Audubon Society; Caw Caw Interpretive Center is run by the Charleston parks department; and Hitchcock Woods is an expansive forest in Aiken that is governed by a non-profit organization.

There is so much to see and do in South Carolina—don't overlook what is right in your own backyard!

PIEDMONT/MOUNTAINS

Geologists believe that millions of years ago the Blue Ridge was the tallest mountain range in the world, rising even higher than today's Mount Everest. Today, the Blue Ridge has weathered into a gently-rolling mountain range that creeps into South Carolina via our Piedmont mountains. What is left, however, are some interesting geological formations, beautiful waterfalls, relic plant communities, an area classified as a temperate rainforest, and much more that begs for exploration. The mountains are moderate enough to welcome visitors year-round, whether to witness dazzling springtime ephemeral displays or autumn hawk migrations that can consist of more than 12,000 raptors in one day.

CAESARS HEAD STATE PARK

8155 Geer Highway
Cleveland, SC 29635
Greenville County
southcarolinaparks.com/caesarshead

When driving up the twisty roads to Caesars Head State Park, visitors receive teasing views of the Blue Ridge Escarpment stretching out below them, but nothing quite equals the grandiose view waiting at the top. At 3,208 feet above sea level, Caesars Head State Park offers panoramic views, and unlike other parks, it does not require a strenuous hike to take in this spectacle. The visitors' center for Caesars Head is located directly above a large cliff, and a short, paved trail leads to a phenomenal outlook point. Many mountains, including the bald head of Table Rock and the sharp peak of Pinnacle Mountain, are visible from this vantage point.

TO DO:  　　**FEE: YES**

Caesars Head State Park is nestled in the Mountain Bridge Wilderness Area with the state's only cove hardwood forest, a botanically diverse type of forest with a large variety of trees and shrubs. This area has elevations ranging from 1,400 to 3,260 feet and contains over 10,000 acres of mountainous terrain. Since Caesars Head State Park is adjacent to the North Carolina border, its forest system is closer in similarity to those found in more northern states. Yellow buckeye, eastern hemlock, white basswood, and magnolia acuminate are among the trees that populate this forest. Also in the Mountain Bridge Wilderness Area is Jones Gap State Park, and it is possible for visitors to hike between the parks. More information about the flora and fauna of the Mountain Bridge Wilderness Area can be found beginning on page 32 where Jones Gap State Park is described.

Hiking is a popular activity in the park, and there are many choices for the day hiker. Raven Cliff Falls is one of the most rewarding treks in the park, as the two-mile path leads down to the spectacular 420-foot waterfall. This waterfall has multiple cascades and is especially beautiful in autumn when fall color is at its peak. A number of other waterfalls are accessible through trails in the park. Waterfalls are plentiful here as this area of the Blue Ridge escarpment has an abrupt 2,000-foot drop to the Piedmont region.

For those who want to see Raven Cliff Falls from a unique viewpoint, the Naturaland Trust Trail is ideal. This trail crosses over Raven Cliff Falls on a suspension bridge and has a second viewpoint of these falls from under a wooden shelter. "The Cathedral" is one of the other spectacular sights on the trail. This tall rock wall with jagged cliffs is more than 200 feet tall and is often dripping with water. The trail is tough and includes several ladders over particularly steep, rocky terrain. It is a much longer and more difficult trail than the Raven Cliff Falls Trail. There are, however, other less difficult trails at Caesars Head, which, due to its expansive size—7,467 acres—has trails of many different lengths and levels.

For those interested in geological features, the Bill Kimball Trail offers impressive views of El Lieutenant, a 300-foot granite rock outcropping that has been compared to Yosemite's El Capitan—although it's not nearly as grandiose. This trail, however, is also fairly difficult, with jagged rocks and steep slopes.

For those looking for a short hike, the Devils Kitchen Trail leaves from the

The profile of Caesar's head, from which the park is said to have received its name, peeks out from a rocky cliff along the Devils Kitchen trail.

Caesars Head overlook and literally takes hikers into the mountain. Devils Kitchen is a natural crack in the giant granite rock that makes up the overlook of Caesars Head. The state park has put stairs through Devils Kitchen to allow visitors to walk through it with ease. Also along this trail is a granite structure that looks like a head—Caesar's head—from which the park received its name. This trail, while brief, offers a variety of interesting features.

The best time to visit Caesars Head is between September and November when the annual hawk migration takes place. Hawks migrating to Central and South America pass through Caesars Head to take advantage of the area's thermals—rising currents of warm air that are common in sudden elevation changes. These birds travel through specific flyways, or paths, that are conducive to their flight due to air currents. Updrafts and thermals in the escarpment are particularly advantageous to hawk flights, and hawks may circle here in large groups known as kettles to gain elevation and then launch into a current that will help carry them on their journey. In September 2014, there were 12,044 hawks recorded in just two days at the park, a phenomenal number of raptors to see at one time. Mid-September is the best time to see hawk migrations. While the number seen in 2014 is unusual, it is not uncommon to see several hundred in one morning during migration periods. Hawkcount.org provides information about the numbers of hawks sighted from September through November on any given day in the park.

Broad-winged hawks are the most frequently sighted hawks in the area,

Even on a winter day, there is still plenty of green at Caesars Head with a plethora of rhododendron and mountain laurel in the park.

but the rare peregrine falcon was reintroduced to the region in the 1980s and can also be sighted here. The peregrine falcon was once endangered due to pesticide overuse, but it has since rebounded. However, even though it has been removed from the endangered species list, it is still rare to spot it in this region.

In the streams throughout Caesars Head State Park resides the federally endangered green salamander, a green and black spotted salamander. South Carolina's largest land animal, the black bear, is a shy creature that is seldom seen but whose population in these mountains is on the rise. Food sources for the bear are plentiful here with an abundance of berries and acorns. Botanically, the rare mountain sweet pitcher plant, a carnivorous plant with blood-red flowers, grows in the Mountain Bridge Area and can be seen from the Pinnacle Pass trail.

Backcountry camping is available for those who want to spend more than one day exploring the park. The park has created hike-in/hike-out sites with fire pits. These sites are rustic and therefore have no water or electrical hookups. Those with a fishing license may also fish for brook, rainbow, and brown trout in the Middle Saluda River, a scenic river that flows through Caesars Head State Park.

GOOD TO KNOW

NEARBY ATTRACTIONS:
Nine Times Heritage Preserve is located near the intersection of Highway 11 and 178 on Eastatoe Creek Road. This preserve has a good display of wildflowers and many songbirds.

DuPont State Forest is located just 15 minutes away, across the North Carolina border, and contains impressive waterfalls, such as Triple Falls. This is one of the most spectacular waterfall destinations near South Carolina.

Bald Rock Heritage Preserve is just five miles from the park and is a large rock outcropping that is perfect for enjoying panoramic views of the mountains and sunsets.

OPTIMAL TIME TO VISIT:
September to November to observe migrating hawks and see fall color at its peak.

WHAT'S UNUSUAL:
Amazing panoramic views; thousands of migrating hawks.

BRING:
Binoculars.

CHAU RAM COUNTY PARK

**1220 Chau Ram Park Road
Westminster, SC 29693
Oconee County
oconeecountry.com/chaurampark**

Chau Ram County Park is quietly nestled at the base of South Carolina's Piedmont mountains, overshadowed by the more popular state parks that pull most visitors to the upstate. What it lacks in prominence, however, this park more than makes up for in its scenery. There are plenty of waterfalls, two scenic rivers, a suspension bridge, and a verdant forest that call to visitors.

TO DO: 🥾 ⛺ 🎣 🛶 🔭 🏊   **FEE: YES**

Located on 244 acres in Westminster, this park is well suited to families. Children delight in splashing in the Chauga River, which beckons bathers with its sandy shoreline and many shallow pools. With elevations that gently roll and dip, there are several pleasant hiking trails that provide scenic views in a pleasant oak and pine forest.

Oconee County is renowned for its numerous waterfalls—some estimate that there are more than 300 located within the county's 626 square miles. They are plentiful in the Piedmont due to the sudden fall in elevation as the Blue Ridge Mountains abruptly rise up from the Sandhills region of the state. The rivers often cut deep gorges into the mountains, exposing rocky shoals and creating lush mountain cove forests and other micro-habitats. Chau Ram provides a great opportunity to experience some of these natural wonders.

Nothing is hidden or difficult to locate at Chau Ram, whose name reflects the monikers of the Chauga and Ramsey rivers that course through it. Immediately upon arriving at the park, visitors delight in a 40-foot waterfall cascading over several granite terraces next to the main parking lot. Here, Ramsey Creek makes a dramatic entrance before joining the Chauga River as it tumbles and flows throughout the park. Even though Ramsey Creek is a smaller waterway,

the granite boulders and surrounding vegetation create a picturesque view that demands appreciation. In the pond below the falls, visitors can sometimes find crayfish, salamanders, waterbugs, and even caddisfly larvae that disguise themselves as watersticks on river bottoms.

The park is favored by locals for its bountiful water activities. Although the Chauga River is only about 24 miles long, it is considered one of the most scenic and spectacular rivers in the state. One of the best places to see this river is from above, which can be achieved by crossing Oconee County's longest suspension bridge. This bridge leads to a variety of paths, including two that parallel the river for a bit. Children enjoy bouncing along this bridge, able to feel its gentle sway as they cross the 160-foot span.

The Chauga River flows relatively calmly through Chau Ram, with several mini-falls that are enjoyable to ride in kayaks, canoes, and even inner tubes. Whereas some parts of the river meander so slowly that visitors might find themselves touching the riverbed in shallow areas, other

Lobelias and other wildflowers are plentiful along the trails at Chau Ram County Park.

parts of the river have small cascades that provide exhilaration. There are four major sets of rapids that can be easily undertaken by most individuals. Anyone wishing to avoid the rapids, however, can portage around them. The Pump House and Can Opener rapids are considered the most challenging in the park; one is located above the suspension bridge, and the other below it.

As with all wild rivers, caution should be used on the river. Life jackets are strongly recommended, and Chau Ram

Park provides some of these, free of charge, hanging up near the bridge entrance. It is necessary to bring your own tubes and boats to the park, and there are no lifeguards on duty, so exercise caution. Because the duration of the river through the park is short, it is possible to walk along the water's edge to view the rapids beforehand.

If watersports are not part of the equation, the river is equally enjoyable from the shore. A sandy path runs along the entire edge of the Chauga River as it navigates its way through Chau Ram Park. Granite boulders dot the perimeter, providing plenty of chances to view the river as well as cool one's feet in its refreshing waters. It is common for locals to picnic here during the summer months, offering a cool respite from the summer heat. The river also is a good place to cast a line for rainbow or brown trout, chubs, bream, and bass.

The park has about four miles of trails, suitable for most hiking levels. Several paths traverse the park's ridges and hills, exposing some of the smaller waterfalls and forest overlooks. The trails crisscross each other as they wind around the hillsides. A stroll in the spring will reveal an array of springtime ephemerals, from dwarf-crested

GOOD TO KNOW

NEARBY ATTRACTIONS:

OPTIMAL TIME TO VISIT:
In the summer to enjoy everything the park has to offer: swimming, tubing, kayaking, and hiking.

WHAT'S UNUSUAL:
A small county park that features waterfalls, easy rapids on which to tube or kayak, and CCC-era cabin ruins.

BRING:
Water, a bathing suit, and possibly a tube.

irises and nodding trilliums to maple-leafed arrowroot and fire-pink flowers that are a favorite among hummingbirds. Equally enticing is an autumn jaunt which showcases a variety of asters alongside the paths.

The blue-blazed Upper Loop heads upstream on the Chauga River, and visitors can see Pump House Rapids near where the city of Westminster has a water intake system. Soon, however, the trail takes a left turn up the mountain, where hikers are transported to a lush mountain forest framed among rhododendrons and other azalea bushes. The purple-hued leather flower, a member of the clematis family that grows wild on hillsides near rivers and streams, also can be found on this trail.

Once atop the mountain, a spur takes visitors to the ruins of the old Scout Cabin. While only a foundation and chimney remain of the cabin—built in the 1930s by the Civilian Conservation Corps—the mountain peak still provides a 180-degree view from the top.

The park was established in 1971 and, in addition to the variety of other activities, it offers camping facilities with showers from March until December. What Chau Ram lacks in size, it more than makes up in beauty and water-based fun. Venture out to the park to discover why it is called one of Oconee County's best kept secrets.

A variety of mushrooms, including boletes, and wildflowers decorate the hillsides of Chau Ram County Park after a rainfall.

CROFT STATE PARK

450 Croft State Park Road
Spartanburg, SC 29302
Spartanburg County
southcarolinaparks.com/croft

Croft State Park is one of the largest in the State Park System and is widely acclaimed for its diversity, attracting a variety of visitors who come to enjoy horseback riding, bike trails, and water-related activities. There are even those who come to probe the foxhole remnants of what was once a major army training facility and German prisoner of war camp during World War II. While Croft is only 20 minutes from Spartanburg's downtown, you'll need a good pair of hiking boots, a mountain bike, or a horse to fully take in all this 7,000-acre park has to offer.

TO DO: 🚶 ⛺ 🎣 🛶 🔭 🏇 📷 📖 🚴   FEE: YES

Principal among Croft's offerings are perhaps its stables and 20 miles of horse trails. Croft is one of the few parks that allows horses within its boundaries. It caters to horse enthusiasts by providing stables with more than 50 stalls so that visitors can camp overnight and have a place to shelter their horses. A show ring and a practice ring also are in place, and horse shows are held at the park on the third Saturday of most months, except December and January.

Camp Croft was created in the 1940s as one of four major U.S. Army training facilities. During World War II, 250,000 soldiers were trained at this location, and 900 German prisoners of war were housed here. Croft Park was established in 1949 when the federal government declared the property as surplus and sold it to the state Forestry Department. While most of the army structures were razed, remnants of combat training still remain, including bunkers and foxholes. These are not, however, located on official trails, and thus it is difficult for the general public to find them.

Prior to its wartime use, the land was privately owned and its rivers powered grist mills. The remnants of one of these mills, Foster Mill, is accessible via the 1.5-mile nature trail that winds through the park. The nature trail slowly descends to an area where visitors find an old stone wall covered in moss next to the picturesque Fairforest Creek. The flume that was dug out for the mill also is visible in this area and is dry except during periods of very intense rain. Signage explains the significance of the mill to the area, as well as what the site once looked like.

The nature trail is a short, easy way to see some of the best attributes of the park. It is one of the few trails that is only accessible by foot (mountain bikes and horses are prohibited). The trail is a loop that splits off in two directions, then eventually reconnects. One half of the loop meanders through a typical forest of oaks, sweetgum, and pine trees. Signage along the way helps visitors identify trees such as black walnut trees or red cedars. The other half of the trail ambles along a ridge which provides great views of Fairforest Creek below. Large beech trees are common along this section of the trail, indicative of the wetter terrain. The trail eventually dips down next to the creek, allowing hikers to cool off in its clear, shallow waters.

Another great trail is the Rocky Ridge Trail, one of the hilliest trails in the park,

A gravestone from the Revolutionary War era sits in one of the seven graveyards in Croft.

which brings visitors by large boulders. This trail connects to the Whitestone Spring Trail, less than a mile in length, that takes hikers or horseback riders to Whitestone Spring. A bright yellow tap shoots up artisanal spring water at this spot, creating a small stream that snakes past the stone remnants of a water bottling plant. The foundation of a once prosperous hotel is also in the area.

One of the most popular features of the park is the 165-acre Lake Craig. A boathouse offers jon boats, canoes, and kayaks—all of which are a great way to explore the lake. Fishing is allowed, but swimming is not. The park will even loan fishing equipment, free of charge, to those interested in fishing for bass, bream, crappie, and catfish. The park's smaller Lake Johnson is another popular fishing destination.

The placid water of Lake Craig beckons paddlers, who frequent the water during warm months.

A pair of bald eagles call Lake Craig home, and during their nesting months from late September through mid-April, it is common to see the birds perched on their nest or soaring nearby. Visitors should not only look to the sky, but also observe the lake for indication that the eagles are soaring about. Hinting at their proximity, ducks and loons will become increasingly nervous, frantically swimming in circles and loudly vocalizing when eagles are overhead. The eagles have lived on the property for nearly five years and have continued to successfully breed.

Something rarely seen in state parks are cemeteries, but Croft has seven graveyards within park boundaries, some of which contain graves from the Revolutionary War era. Many of the older gravestones were made with soft soapstone, and their text has begun to erode away. Some of these burial sites can be seen from the Foster Mills Trail, a 6.5-mile hike that takes you along ridges, across an old trestle bridge, and along the shore of Lake Craig.

The Palmetto Trail also runs through the park. The trail's slogan is "From Mountains to Sea," which alludes to the fact that this trail, when complete, will traverse the entire state of South Carolina from the coast to the Blue Ridge Mountains. About 12.5 miles of the trail wind through the park. It is along this trail that visitors can find the foundations of homesteads that pre-date World War II.

One of the most popular trails in the park is the Fairforest Creek Trail. This trail takes visitors to a 65-foot expansion bridge, the longest expansion bridge in the State Park System. This fiberglass bridge crosses the creek at one of its widest spots, with no supporting beams, and is considered the "gateway to the mountain biking trails." More than 10 miles of mountain biking trails, ranging in difficulty, lie beyond the bridge. Motorcycles created a few of the trails in the '70s and '80s, some of which are fall line trails, meaning they drop to the bottom of a slope as quickly as possible. Many of the trails also have jumps, for the more daring mountain biker; however, bypasses are frequent around the difficult parts. Along the river, look for mountain laurel, wild bamboo, river birch trees, and many different types of mushrooms, which thrive in the rich, damp soil.

Croft is an urban oasis, offering outdoor enthusiasts a myriad of activities within minutes of city limits. Visitors can hike, bike, and ride amongst the white-tailed deer that frequent the park, or feel a sense of history offered by the many stone remnants dating back as early as the 1700s. It is the epitome of the wonders that the State Park System offers—history, nature, and wonderful outdoor activities.

GOOD TO KNOW

NEARBY ATTRACTIONS:
Sumter National Forest contains more than 350,000 acres within its bounds and offers extensive trail systems, mountain biking, hunting, and equestrian activities.

Edwin M. Griffin Nature Preserve, also known as the Cottonwood Trail, is a 115-acre preserve located near downtown Spartanburg. Lawson's Fork Creek runs through the park, and offers hiking as well as paddling opportunities.

Glendale Shoals Preserve offers hiking and boating opportunities along Lawson's Fork. One of the most picturesque sites of the park is a spillway that cascades below a rustic metal bridge.

OPTIMAL TIME TO VISIT:
In the fall, winter, and spring to avoid the heat.

WHAT'S UNUSUAL:
So many different activities within the confines of a state park.

BRING:
Water and a bike.

DEVILS FORK STATE PARK

161 Holcombe Circle
Salem, SC 29676
Oconee and Pickens counties
southcarolinaparks.com/devilsfork

South Carolina's landscape is bursting with lakes, the vast majority of which are manmade, and residents are fortunate that every major reservoir touches a state park. In 1973, a state partnership with Duke Power Company created Lake Jocassee when the area was dammed and flooded, creating a pristine Piedmont recreational lake and a hydroelectric dam. Today, the only public access to this lake is at Devils Fork State Park, a 644-acre park in the heart of Jocassee Gorges that has a variety of unusual plants, including one very rare native.

TO DO: 🚶 ⛺ 🎣 🛶 🔭 📷 🏊 🏠   **FEE: YES**

The lure of the park is primarily its large, unspoiled lake. The 7,500-acre reservoir is about 300 feet deep and is fed by clean mountain streams that keep it cold and clear throughout the entire year. Boating is a popular activity on this lake, and while the state park has no public power boats available for rent, it does have four boat ramps for those who bring their own watercraft. Additionally, nearby off-site companies rent pontoons, jet skis, and motorboats. It is also possible to rent paddleboards, canoes, and kayaks through a private company on the state park property. Lake Jocassee is one of the state's most undeveloped lakes with 75 miles of preserved shoreline; however, its many waterfalls and streams are not easily accessible by foot.

Most spectacular is the 80-foot-high Laurel Creek Falls. By foot, this area is only accessible via a 16-mile round trip trek up and down mountains; by boat, it is minutes away. The falls have three tiers, and two views are available from the lake: a frontal view from the end of the cove or a profile view from a closer standpoint. Visitors often swim at the second level in a small pool. Also optional is a short hike to the top of the falls, which is accessible by a mile-long trail that begins at the mouth of the cove. This trail provides a nice view of the lake and is worth the hike.

In the past, multi-year droughts have significantly lowered lake levels at Devils Fork, which sometimes makes it necessary to dock farther away from the falls and trail. Although the water levels have varied significantly over the years, the lake is deep enough that it is always navigable, even when precipitation levels are low.

Lake Jocassee is so unusually clear that it often piques the interest of scuba divers. Private scuba shops in the area offer certification and dives. Underwater visibility extends from 15 to 50 feet, and temperatures range from around 80 degrees in the summer to 50 in the winter. One popular trip includes a visit to the now-underwater Mount Carmel cemetery, which was the filming site of the movie *Deliverance* in 1972 before the creation of the lake. While the flooding of the reservoir led to the demolishment of most structures, a completely intact lodge was recently discovered on the lake floor.

As it is a lake fed by clear, cool mountain streams, Lake Jocassee offers prime fishing opportunities. The lake contains trophy trout and smallmouth bass as well as brown trout, rainbow

The Oconee bell is a rare flower of the Southern Appalachians.

GOOD TO KNOW

NEARBY ATTRACTIONS:

Whitewater Falls, across the North Carolina border, is the highest waterfall east of the Rockies and has great hiking trails.

Eastatoe Creek Heritage Preserve has an old growth forest with hemlock, rare ferns, salamanders, and other interesting plants and animals.

Caesars Head State Park (page 12)

Table Rock State Park (page 68)

Stumphouse Mountain Tunnel and Yellow Branch Falls (page 64)

Chau Ram Park (page 16)

OPTIMAL TIME TO VISIT:
In the spring to see the rare Oconee bell flower; in the summer to enjoy boating and swimming at the park; in the fall for colorful foliage.

WHAT'S UNUSUAL:
Lake Jocassee has more than 70 miles of shoreline and waterfalls easily reached by hiking. The park is the only public access to this pristine lake. Devils Fork also has a good population of the rare Oconee bell flowers.

BRING:
A bathing suit.

trout, white bass, largemouth bass, bluegill, and black crappie.

On land, Jocassee has other interesting sites. The Oconee Bell Trail, which takes off from the visitors' center parking lot, is a short one-mile hike that winds through a hardwood forest. From mid-March to early April, the trail is a prime location from which to view a large colony of rare, wild Oconee bells.

Oconee bells are recognizable by their white and pinkish flowers that resemble nodding bells hovering over shiny green leaves tinged in red. The plant was originally discovered in Oconee County in 1788 by a French botanist, but confusing maps and descriptions led others to believe the plant had become extinct. In 1839, American botanist Asa Gray began a lifelong quest to find the flower; he ultimately failed, and the plant was not located for nearly 30 years more. In May 1877, a 17-year-old boy named George McQueen Hyams of Statesville, NC, brought the unknown plant to his father, an amateur botanist. It was confirmed as *shortia galacifolia*, the long-lost Oconee bell.

The plant thrives along streambeds and on the slopes of gorges, enjoying areas of high rainfall. It is believed that the species was nearly wiped out when the gorge was dammed and flooded to create Lake Jocassee. Thus, walking

Devils Fork State Park is the only public access to the 7,500-acre Lake Jocassee, a popular boating destination.

along this short nature trail is particularly worthwhile.

The park's only other official trail is a two-mile loop that affords occasional views of the lake. The trail is hilly, and it passes through a mixed hardwood forest of dogwood, black cherry, red maple, and a variety of other trees. In the early spring, Oconee bells also can be found in some areas of this trail, as can orange-colored chanterelle mushrooms.

While the park is limited in its hikes, its prime location in the Jocassee Gorge affords many day trips to other significant sites and hikes. The Jocassee Gorge area was featured in a special edition of *National Geographic*'s magazine,

"50 of the World's Last Great Places— Destinations of a Lifetime" in 2012. From Whitewater Falls to Stumphouse Mountain Tunnel (page 64), there are plenty of sites to visit in this unique area of the state.

Devils Fork State Park opened in 1991 and is one of the newer additions to the State Park System. As such, it has some of the most pristine state park cabins, built in cooperation with Duke Energy, many of which contain expansive windows overlooking the scenic lake. These cabins make Devils Fork State Park the perfect place to stay for a few days and explore the many parks, waterfalls, heritage preserves, and other attractions in the upstate.

FORTY ACRE ROCK HERITAGE PRESERVE

2207 Conservancy Road
Kershaw, SC 29067
Lancaster County

Visiting Forty Acre Rock Heritage Preserve is akin to traveling back in time. The park's namesake, a massive exposed rock, harbors bright-colored plant life that, combined with the emptiness of the granite dome, creates a prehistoric sensibility. While the granite rock is the focal point of the 2,267-acre site, other interesting features make this one of South Carolina's unique habitats and a must-see destination.

TO DO: **FEE: NO**

The moniker, Forty Acre Rock, is a bit misleading: the exposed rock section is only 14 acres in size. In reality, however, the rock actually extends well beyond the exposed tip, surpassing the 40-acre tag. Thus, either way you look at it, the name is incorrect.

There are two designated parking lots to access Forty Acre Rock. A 1.5-mile trail connects these two lots and provides two main sites of interest along the way: a small beaver pond and Forty Acre Rock. The lot accessed via Conservancy Road is closer to Forty Acre Rock, while the other parking lot is nearer to the beaver pond. Because the lot accessed via Conservancy Road is easier to find, and is considered the main address of the preserve, it is recommended. Trails are marked via plaques, which are helpful as it can be easy to get lost at Forty Acre Rock due to its wide expanse.

Forty Acre Rock was created by magma that cooled deep below Earth's surface and was later exposed by erosion. While similar environments are frequently mined for granite, Forty Acre Rock was saved from this fate by its granite's low quality. Along the lower edge of the rock, a deep cut is evidence of granite mining, done before the rocks were deemed too poor to use. Additionally, visitors who look closely can see damage from where lightning struck the rock, resulting in small circles that dot its surface.

Greenish-blue lichen and black moss cover the granite in patches, creating a picturesque blotchy surface. Cedars pop up amongst the rocks, and many have been thriving for hundreds of years. The true draw of the preserve, however, are the unique plant species that sprout from the small pools that form from rainwater collected in granite depressions. The water level in these pools is always uncertain, and thus plants must be able to adapt to extremely dry or wet conditions in order to survive here. Further, because these pools are so spatially separate from the forest surrounding Forty Acre Rock, unique species found in very few places in the world make their home here. Just as the Galapagos Islands' isolation created individual species, the pools in Forty Acre Rock do as well. Among these is Small's stonecrop, a waxy bright red plant with small stalks that stands out on the grey speckled rock. Take time to peer at these plants up close: these dwarfed forests will impress!

The bright colors of the plants on Forty Acre Rock are what make this preserve

The red-bellied woodpecker is one of a half dozen woodpeckers that can be found in the area.

so striking. Woolly ragwort's bright yellow flowers, pineweed's vibrant green stalks, and pool sprite's snowy flowers all contrast intensely against the unique grey backdrop that the rock offers. Most of these plants are annuals and thus flower and seed once a year before perishing.

A small but picturesque waterfall sits directly below the large granite outcropping that is Forty Acre Rock. There is a short, narrow path that leads to this waterfall on the bottom left side. Visitors must follow the left side of the rock down to find the path, which is fairly steep but short. It branches into separate paths: one that leads to the base of the waterfall and a small cave decorated with spray paint. The other leads to the top of the waterfall, which has several small cascades that flow down a flat rock. The waterfalls flow during all seasons, yet particularly dry periods can, of course, completely stop the water flow.

Another landmark on the preserve is Devil's Footprint, a depression on the lower right end of the rock that is shaped like a cloven footprint. The print looks as if it was seared into the rock by the Devil's fiery spirit and can be fairly difficult to find without the aid of someone who is familiar with its location.

Surrounding the large granite outcropping of Forty Acre Rock is a long- and shortleaf pine forest. Loblolly pines were planted in the area after logging decimated the short- and longleaf pines; however, the preserve is transitioning back to its original state.

Black and white warblers and phoebes make their home in the forest, as do red-bellied woodpeckers and migrating yellow-bellied sapsuckers. A side sandy path winds through this forest, which is open to foot traffic only. (Vehicles are prohibited in the area because they disturb the fragile ecosystems in the pools.) Likewise, visitors should always walk around these pools.

There is an active beaver population within the preserve that can be viewed from the small pond that the path winds around. While beavers tend to be nocturnal, their wooden dams are usually visible, as are the tell-tale gnawings on area trees. A wooden footbridge passes over this pond, which is covered in a blanket of water lilies and is lush and beautiful. The pond is surrounded by a hardwood forest that is home to white-tailed deer and more songbirds.

Although not a designated trail within the preserve, a walkable roadway—part of the old Highway 601—begins at a metal gate at the far end of the preserve. The old highway was abandoned because of its curvy nature, which led to many wrecks. This broad pathway leads across Flat Creek, a muddy stream surrounded by moss banks. In the spring, wildflowers

GOOD TO KNOW

OPTIMAL TIME TO VISIT:
In the spring—late March to mid-April—to see wildflowers in bloom and brightly colored plants in rock depressions, preferably after recent rains.

WHAT'S UNUSUAL:
Rare plant species and a large granite outcropping.

BRING:
Water.

such as spring beauties, bloodroot, wild ginger, and nodding trilliums grow rampant here. Bloodroot has distinctive large white flowers, but its name was derived from its red roots, which were used as a dye by Native Americans. This pathway stretches on for miles, but these beautiful flowers can be found within the first mile of the former road.

While there is not an extensive trail system within Forty Acre Rock Preserve, it is a truly remarkable piece of land with unusual plant life that is seldom seen any other place in South Carolina.

JONES GAP STATE PARK

303 Jones Gap Road
Marietta, SC 29661
Greenville County
southcarolinaparks.com/jonesgap

Nestled in the Mountain Bridge Wilderness area, Jones Gap State Park is a favorite destination for many South Carolinians, with its boisterous creeks, plentiful waterfalls, and surplus of inspiring trails. This 3,946-acre park has the most extensive trail system in the state, each one as beautiful as the next, providing varied hiking opportunities suitable for all hiking levels.

TO DO:    **FEE: YES**

Located right below the North Carolina/ South Carolina border, Jones Gap and Caesars Head state parks make up the Mountain Bridge Wilderness area. This zone has elevations ranging from 1,400 to 3,260 feet and contains more than 10,000 acres of mountainous terrain.

The forest in Jones Gap State Park is an overlap between two separate forest systems: a "cover hardwood forest" more common in North Carolina, and an oak-hickory forest that is common to the South Carolina Piedmont. Typical trees of the former include yellow buckeye, eastern hemlock, white basswood, and *magnolia acuminata*—one of the largest and most cold-hardy magnolias, often referred to as the "cucumber tree" due to the color and shape of its unripe fruit.

The area's moist, boggy soils contribute to a profusion of ferns and wildflowers, some of which are rare, such as dutchman's pipe, blue cohosh, and walking fern. In the spring, a ranger often leads wildflower walks, providing the opportunity to explore the many varieties of blooming flowers. The park is also home to expansive swaths of poison ivy, so visitors should stay on trails and be on guard for this woody vine that bears three distinctive leaflets.

The land for Jones Gap was not brought into the State Park System until 1989, making it a fairly recent addition. Its young age, however, is no reflection on the grandeur of the park. With its abundance of waterfalls, over 30 miles of hiking trails, swimming and fishing opportunities, and unusual plants, Jones Gap is teeming with possibilities.

The first state-owned fish hatchery was developed on the land around Jones Gap in the 1800s, and a small display and trout pond sit adjacent to the visitors' center as a tribute to these origins. Although this current trout pond is purely educational, Jones Gap still offers some of the best fishing in the state. The Middle Saluda River, the state's first designated scenic river, runs through the park and contains brook, rainbow, and brown trout. A scenic river is one that has been recognized because of its unique and important features, and thus the state is heavily involved in protecting it. The best opportunity to meander along the Middle Saluda River is along the five-mile Jones Gap trail, but be prepared to cross the stream at several locations.

A variety of salamanders call the Middle Saluda River home. Recent rainfalls will bring these amphibians to the edge of streambeds and pathways. During drier times, look beneath

The picturesque Rainbow Falls, one of several cascades within the park, seldom disappoints hikers.

Granite boulders at Jones Gap dominate many paths and are cleverly incorporated into hiking trails.

There really is no bad time of year to visit Jones Gap. In the spring, high levels of rain create dense, lush vegetation. Moss grows on the rocks that dot the Middle Saluda River, and wildflowers bloom on the side of the trail. In the summer, the cool water of the river beckons visitors to take a dip in perfectly-sized swimming holes. In autumn, tree leaves turn brilliant shades of red, orange, and yellow, creating a spectacular canvas of color. In the winter, the abundance of mountain laurel and rhododendron in the lower elevation areas give the park a sense of life despite little else being green. On the higher elevation trails, hikers can see though gaps created by bare limbs and glimpse views of the peaks of the Mountain Bridge Wilderness Area that are obscured by foliage during other seasons.

moist leaves or under rocks and logs to spot one of these creatures, though do not handle them as they are very susceptible to disease. Black-bellied salamanders, Oconee salamanders, red-spotted newts, and other types of amphibians thrive in Jones Gap's waters. Crawdads also are abundant. The park is a designated Audubon Bird Sanctuary, and numerous migratory birds live here as well.

Jones Gap has a number of interesting geological features. Among these is Hospital Rock, a boulder as large as a house that forms a shelter. (It is rumored that a Confederate soldier hid under Hospital Rock during the Civil War.) Because the trail is considered strenuous, it is often delightfully underpopulated. The trail to Hospital Rock also offers glimpses of Cleveland Cliffs: tall rock walls with jagged edges that are a wonder to see. On the Rim of the Gap trail, visitors pass through Weight Watchers Rock, a group of rocks with an opening so narrow hikers might consider the need to alter their diets. In reality, the opening is adequate to allow most to pass through it, and there is an alternative means around the impediment.

Due to some drastic changes in topography, Jones Gap has a glut of waterfalls. The trails showcasing some of these natural wonders also are exceptional. Experience Silver Steps Falls, Buckeye Falls, Dargans Cascades, Falls Creek Falls, Rainbow Falls, and Jones Gap Falls at this park. Each of these waterfalls is beautiful; however, Rainbow Falls and Falls Creek Falls are the largest and most spectacular.

GOOD TO KNOW

NEARBY ATTRACTIONS:

Bald Rock Heritage Preserve (page 15)

Caesars Head State Park (page 12)

Nine Times Heritage Preserve (page 15)

OPTIMAL TIME TO VISIT:
Each season has something unique to offer.

WHAT'S UNUSUAL:
The plethora of salamanders and waterfalls, an expansive trail system, and a hardwood forest more common in North Carolina.

BRING:
Water and a bathing suit.

NOTE: There is limited parking at the park, so make sure to arrive early in the morning during the busy season!

KEOWEE TOXAWAY STATE PARK

**108 Residence Drive
Sunset, SC 29685
Pickens County
southcarolinaparks.com/keoweetoxaway**

Keowee Toxaway State Park sits on the edge of the Jocassee Gorges, a beautiful, untamed region in the northwest corner of South Carolina and over the border into North Carolina. Because of its natural beauty, in 2012 the National Geographic Society included the area on its list of "50 of the World's Last Great Places" in the "Destinations of a Lifetime" edition of the magazine. The Gorges received this designation due to the plethora of waterfalls found in the region.

TO DO: 🚶 ⛺ 🎣 🛶 🏊 🏠   **FEE: YES**

The gushing waterfalls are a byproduct of the plentiful rainfall here, which is among the highest of any place in the United States. These waterways help feed the main attraction of Keowee Toxaway—its 18,000-acre lake that is the park's cornerstone.

The Keowee Toxaway State Park visitors' center serves as a welcome center for the entire Jocassee Gorges region and provides information about the natural landscape and history of the area. Signage in the visitors' center explains the area's history and what makes it spectacular—its wildness. The area overflows with flowers and miles of thick, lush forests. Approximately 43,500 acres of protected land make up the region, and in addition to its beauty, the area contains incredible resources, including several important watersheds.

While the visitors' center provides a great introduction to the area, the best way to get a grasp on its wonder is to explore the trails. The two main trails are accessible via the parking area adjacent to the visitors' center. The Natural Bridge Trail is a 1.3-mile loop trail named for the large, natural stone bridge that crosses Poe Creek. Rhododendron borders the creek, as do wildflowers such as

trout lily, bloodroot, and violets. This trail connects to the Raven Rock Trail, a 4.4-mile loop that snakes towards the shore of Lake Keowee. The trail meanders alongside the clear water of Lake Keowee, changing elevation to take hikers to the tops of rocky cliffs with great views of the lake.

Alongside the Raven Rock Trail are three backcountry camping sites that only can be accessed by hiking or by canoe. Each campsite, with its adjoining fire ring, sits on the shore of Lake Keowee, providing a spectacular view. Campsites with electrical hookups and restroom facilities are available closer to the visitors' center, and the park also offers a lakeside three-bedroom cabin with modern amenities.

While the park only has 5.5 miles of trails, the terrain that they navigate varies dramatically. The Natural Bridge

Cascades within the park help feed its cornerstone 18,000-acre lake.

Rhododendron and mountain laurel grow abundantly at Keowee-Toxaway, adding to the lushness of the landscape year-round.

Trail begins in a hardwood forest dominated by oaks and hickories. Chanterelle mushrooms pop up rampantly in this forest after periods of heavy rain, and their bright orange hue offers a burst of color to the forest floor. The trail begins at a relatively high elevation, and as it gives way to

the Raven Rock Trail, the elevation drops—an indication that the sparkling turquoise lake is getting nearer.

The variety of soil in the park offers intrigue as the trails change from black dirt to red clay. While the dirt provides a soft barrier to treading feet, the clay adds something unique to the park. The lake is lined in this orange clay, which makes for fantastic water. The thick clay is not churned up as easily as dirt is and helps the water remain clearer. Along the trail, the clay perfectly preserves animal tracks in its dense solidity. Lucky visitors might see a black bear or raccoon print trapped within the clay, a reminder that humans share the land with these wild creatures.

Water, as it turns out, is the ingredient that makes this park sparkle. When Raven Rock Trail meanders away from the lake, it reconnects again with Poe Creek. It is here that moss grows profusely on smooth rocks that border rippling water. There are many opportunities to cool off among these creeks, such as where Raven Rock Trail meets up with the Natural Bridge Trail. Here, a small, picturesque waterfall sits right off the trail. This is an understated example of the variety of waterfalls found within the Jocassee Gorges. (Taller,

GOOD TO KNOW

NEARBY ATTRACTIONS:
Laurel Fork Heritage Preserve, on Laurel Fork Gap Road near Sunset, has more than 1,300 acres of mountainous terrain with river gorges, waterfalls, and the diverse plant life that accompanies this ecosystem.

OPTIMAL TIME TO VISIT:
In the summer to experience all the water-based fun.

WHAT'S UNUSUAL:
So much water and a natural bridge.

BRING:
A bathing suit and a kayak.

more intense waterfalls can be found in other natural areas throughout Oconee and Pickens counties.) Nevertheless, there is something calm and peaceful about running water, and it is a beautiful sight, especially on a warm day.

Even though the Jocassee Gorges are celebrated for their wild beauty, human activity is prevalent throughout the park. The lake itself is manmade and is a popular destination for boaters. Motor boats speed across the lake, sometimes towing tubes or water-skiers. Across from the park, expensive homes dot the shorelines, and a golf course graces the lake's edge. Even with this encroachment of human activity, the lake is beautiful, the views are outstanding, and lushness abounds on trails and shores.

Keowee Toxaway is one of the best places to enjoy a family-centric, fun-filled day. There is a decent amount of mileage to explore, several different swimming options, and good places to canoe or kayak. Visitors should come out and explore what makes this park glisten.

KINGS MOUNTAIN STATE PARK

1277 Park Road
Blacksburg, SC 29702
York County
southcarolinaparks.com/
  kingsmountain

KINGS MOUNTAIN NATIONAL MILITARY PARK

2625 Park Road
Blacksburg, SC 29702
York County
nps.gov/kimo

A common misconception is that "Kings Mountain" refers to a single peak when it is actually the name given to the entire Kings Mountain Range, a 16-mile-long expanse of low peaks that runs through both North and South Carolina. Just as there is not only one mountain worth noting in the Kings range, there is more than one park worth exploring here as well. Kings Mountain State Park and Kings Mountain National Military Park are located just below the North Carolina border, west of Charlotte, and offer distinct experiences at their locations.

TO DO: 🥾 ⛺ 🎣 🛶 🏊 🔭 📷 📖 🏇 🏠 🚴 **FEE: YES**

Kings Mountain State Park offers a multitude of trails, a working 19th-century demonstration farm, and more historic Civilian Conservation Corps-built structures than any other park in South Carolina. It has a typical Piedmont hardwood forest, although there are many less common upstate plants, such as mountain laurel and rhododendrons. Beech trees, shortleaf pine, and Virginia pine are among the most common trees lining the trails in the park. Whitetail deer, chipmunks, and beavers make their homes in the forest. An orange-blazed trail that runs along Lake Crawford takes visitors to an active beaver dam where bird activity is rampant. Boy Scouts completing an Eagle Scout project constructed an overlook with benches that provide views of the dam.

One of the biggest draws to the state park is the mid-19th century Yeoman-style farm. The farm contains historic buildings that were relocated to the state park. Included among the buildings is historic machinery, such as an apparatus for making sorghum syrup and a cotton gin. The farm also contains animals such as sheep, chickens, and roosters, and visitors can purchase feed for these animals. The entire display is set up as it would have existed in the 1800s, exhibiting crops, fruit trees, and an herb garden. The Farm Trail, a relatively flat 1.5-mile trail, takes visitors from the Lake Crawford bathhouse to the farm through a wooded trail. It crosses several small footbridges and also meanders past the lake, a beautiful stone dam, and a wetlands area.

In the summer months, visitors can rent boats to use in Lake Crawford or bring their own to use on Lake York. Fishing is another popular activity in the park, but is only permitted with a valid fishing license. Early November also is a great time to visit both parks. At this time, fall color is spectacular. While bright leaves have disappeared in most upstate parks this late in the season, fall lasts a little longer here and yellow leaves still cling to the trees. Both parks also offer horseback trails, adding to the nostalgic and historic ambiance. Kings Mountain State Park even offers equestrian campsites in addition to regular campsites. While there are no bike trails, visitors may bike on paved roads.

Although the state park has many natural areas to explore, history runs deep here. Stop by the state park office to pick up literature and marvel at its building, a 1770s cabin that contains much of its original wood. Two families lived in the home before it was converted to the state park office.

Plaques, signs, and memorials dot the Battlefield Trail, explaining the state's significance in the Revolutionary War.

Among the other historic structures at the park are a variety of CCC-built structures, including the two man-made lakes, a picturesque stone dam on the edge of Lake Crawford, and 78 wooden buildings. This noteworthy architecture has allowed Kings Mountain State Park to make the National Register of Historic Places.

Among the largest CCC buildings are the bathhouse on Lake Crawford and a variety of rentable structures that make up two camps. Summer camps or church groups with as many as 200 people frequently occupy these historic cabins, which contain plaques that commemorate the CCC. Camp Cherokee and York Group Camps are both on Lake York and contain a dining hall, sports facilities, and many sleeping cabins. The cabins have the comforting aroma of campfire as those who stay here still use the large fireplaces that are the centerpieces of many of the cabins.

A single paved road runs from Kings Mountain State Park to Kings Mountain National Military Park, allowing visitors to easily drive from one destination to the next. It also is possible to hike between the parks via the Ridgeline Trail. The Ridgeline Trail further links the parks to Crowders Mountain State Park in North Carolina, a nearby park that has great hiking and fall color.

Another option is the Park Loop Trail, a 16-mile trail that explores the perimeter of both the military and state parks. It is a great way to see two parks at once, while staying completely within South Carolina's borders.

Kings Mountain National Military Park is a federally funded park (part of the National Park System) that is most famous for its Revolutionary War history. The park commemorates a battle that took place on October 7, 1780, a victory for the Patriots that is considered a turning point in the Revolutionary War. The most common attraction is the hilly 1.5-mile Battlefield Trail that winds around the undulating landscape. The uneven nature of the battlefield was of great importance during the fight as Patriots were able to surprise British soldiers and Loyalists from above. Many monuments, including two giant stone memorials, dot the trail. Signs detailing events of the battle and famous generals and soldiers in the war educate visitors along the way.

Having an adjoining national and state park is unique, and the proximity allows visitors to explore both parks in one day. Despite being in the same mountain range, the parks have distinct offerings, and each deserves a visit. Experience several trails that wind through forests, fields, and near lakes at Kings Mountain State Park, and take in a bit of Revolutionary War history at Kings Mountain National Military Park. It will be a day well spent.

GOOD TO KNOW

NEARBY ATTRACTIONS:
Crowders Mountain State Park, just across the border in North Carolina, offers great vistas and giant boulders for those looking for a more mountainous hike. Rock climbing also is popular here. The parks are connected by the Ridgeline Trail.

Daniel Stowe Botanical Gardens has 380 acres of spectacular gardens that feature natives and more exotic plants, including a conservatory with tropical plants and orchids.

OPTIMAL TIME TO VISIT:
Early November for great fall color; summer for lake activities.

WHAT'S UNUSUAL:
The historical significance of both parks. Kings Mountain State Park has an unusual amount of CCC-built structures, while Kings Mountain National Military Park offers insight into South Carolina's Revolutionary War history.

BRING:
Water.

LANDSFORD CANAL STATE PARK

2051 Park Drive
Catawba, SC 29704
Chester County
southcarolinaparks.com/landsfordcanal

For six weeks a year, Landsford Canal becomes an enchanted wonderland where 22 acres of rocky shoals spider lilies sparkle among the rock outcroppings of the gently flowing Catawba River. It's an amazing sight to see, and one that is unparalleled anywhere else in the world.

TO DO: 🥾 🎣 🛶 🔭 📷 📖   **FEE: YES**

The rocky shoals spider lily is a member of the amaryllis family but grows only in fast-flowing rivers in Georgia, Alabama, and South Carolina. In recent years, the flower has popped up at the Riverfront Park in Columbia, although not nearly in the multitude that proliferates at Landsford Canal State Park. Altogether, about 60 rocky shoals spider lily communities are known to exist, but the Landsford Canal population is considered the most impressive in both size and density.

The plants require a very specific environment to thrive—a fast moving river. With the ever increasing number of manmade dams and lakes in the state, the habitats for these flowers are in great decline. Consequently, the rocky shoals spider lily is now federally listed as a species of concern.

The spider lily is a perennial that grows about three feet tall. Each bulb, which grows wedged between rocks in a streambed, produces up to three stalks. These stalks will yield about six flowers that each blooms on subsequent days, forming decorative white, star-like flowers that span about six inches. The spider lilies bloom for up to six weeks, but the largest groups blossom from around mid-May to mid-June. Typically, June 1st is the height of the show, yet the state park website keeps an up-to-date "lily watch" that outlines the peak time per season.

Landsford Canal is an otherwise sleepy state park that becomes a popular destination when lilies bloom. From the banks of the river, the best viewing spot is about three-fourths of a mile from the parking lot. A flat, easy trail leads visitors to a viewing platform from which it is possible to see the full expanse of the blooming flowers.

Paths skirt the river and provide views of the old canal system, which dates back to 1819.

An even better way to see the flowers is via canoe or kayak. Unfortunately, the state park system does not have boats available for rent, so visitors must bring their own. The river rapids are considered level I or II, making the trip easily negotiable for most boaters. Following periods of heavy rainfall, however, it can sometimes increase to level III rapids. During May and June, rangers are generally positioned around the welcome area and are effective at gauging the pulse of the river. When the water movement is too strong and dangerous, rangers turn boaters away.

Generally, the biggest issue concerning the Catawba River is not too much water, but too little. Large, heavy canoes tend to bottom out, and even lighter kayaks have been known to scrape the river bottom in shallow areas, necessitating a gentle push or rocking action to help move them on their way. Altogether, the river drops about 32 feet in the two miles that it flows through the park. There is a 1.5-mile canoe trail that leads visitors from the park's entrance to a take-out point. Many people choose to park a car at the entrance and take-out point to avoid excess walking; however, the plethora of signs and trees at the end of the river trail make for excellent places to lock boats, enabling rafters to walk back to the first parking lot to retrieve their cars.

Paddling pays off in big dividends when boaters approach the incredible display of lilies. From the middle of the river, the spider lilies completely surround the boats in a dazzling pageantry of white pinwheels, while red-winged blackbirds flit in and out of their nesting sites among the rocks. Deer sometimes cross

Kayaking on the slow-moving Catawba River is an ideal way to enjoy the splendor of the spider lilies.

the river at midday to nibble on plants, and an occasional banded or red-bellied water snake may swim past.

While it is the lilies that steal most of the attention, these flowers actually had little to do with the state park designation. Landsford Canal State Park was established in 1970 because it is the last remaining preserved canal in the state. History buffs also will appreciate that Thomas Sumter and Colonel William R. Davies used the river as a staging area during the American Revolution.

Landsford Canal was designed during the 19th century to transport cotton from the upcountry down to its export station in Charleston and bypass the rocky section of the river. Only boats that were seven feet wide and designed to float in 18 inches of water could be pulled through the canal. These boats carried up to 50 bales of cotton, the predominant crop in the Piedmont. Construction on the canal began in 1819 and was completed in 1832 through the use of slave and Irish immigrant labor. It had a series of three locks that dropped a combined 32 feet. In addition to the now-empty canals, visitors can see the old locks used to raise and lower water, a miller's house, and a lock keeper's house, although none are in particularly noteworthy shape.

The state's canal system was only utilized until around 1840, and Landsford Canal was never highly regarded. One of the locks collapsed in 1824 due to a poor foundation, and the entire canal system was abandoned when railroads made it obsolete. The land was eventually purchased by Duke Power Company, which in turn donated it to the state.

The path to view the remnants of this canal system is actually the old tow-route used by mules to drag the barges through the water. Altogether, it is a three-mile trip to hike the path and return to the parking lot. This hike, however, is interesting year-round with a variety of plants and animals, including an active bald eagle's nest. (When planning a visit, keep in mind that eagles are born in the winter months and fledge in early spring.) Noteworthy plants include the spring-blooming Carolina silverbell, paw paw trees, and purple spiderwort, all of which grow profusely along the pathways. Also common are Jack-in-the-pulpit, cranefly orchids, Solomon's seal, spicebush, phlox, and columbine, to name a few. Birds are abundant. Neotropical warblers come through during the summer months, while egrets, ducks, and other songbirds remain year-round.

The chance to view about 22 acres of rocky shoals spider lilies should not be missed. Grab a camera and head out to this state park and prepare to be impressed!

GOOD TO KNOW

NEARBY ATTRACTIONS:
Andrew Jackson State Park is a quiet park with two one-mile trails and a lake that offers fishing and paddleboat rentals. It is the birthplace of Andrew Jackson, and it has a museum that houses Revolutionary War artifacts and items related to the seventh president.

Glencairn Gardens in York County is a 10-acre botanical garden with walking paths and bridges that wind through trees, ornamental bushes, and flowers. Peak blooming time is March to April.

OPTIMAL TIME TO VISIT:
April and May to see the flowers in bloom.

WHAT'S UNUSUAL:
The largest known population of rocky shoals spider lilies and remnants of the state's old canal system.

BRING:
Canoes or kayaks and drinking water.

MUSGROVE MILL STATE HISTORIC SITE

398 State Park Road
Clinton, SC 29325
Laurens County
southcarolinaparks.com/musgrovemill

On a tramp through the quiet, rolling Piedmont forests of Musgrove Mill State Historic Site, it is easy to imagine the stalwart but outnumbered Patriots who valiantly defeated British Loyalists during the American Revolution. While history buffs flock to this park for a peek at American history, the park holds interest for others as well, with its varied habitats, popular swimming holes, and canoeing possibilities.

TO DO: 🥾 🛶 🏊 🔭 📷 📖   **FEE: YES**

The park is named for Edward Musgrove, a wealthy backcountry colonist whose property was occupied by British Loyalists—colonial men who were loyal to the British Empire—during the Revolutionary War. Of British descent, Musgrove did not claim allegiance to either the American colonies or Great Britain during the war. It is widely believed that Musgrove's daughter Mary, however, was a courageous Patriot who hid a soldier nicknamed Horseshoe Robinson in a cave under the waterfall that now bears his moniker. Her heroism is said to be the basis of a fictional character who took great personal risks spying for the Patriots in a British 19th-century novel called *Horseshoe Robinson: A Tale of Tory Ascendency*.

Musgrove Mill is a relatively small park with fewer than 400 acres and only about 2.5 miles of maintained trails, but the setting, historical features, and diversity of habitats make for a memorable visit. With the Enoree River ambling through the center of the park and the Piedmont's rolling hills beginning to emerge from the landscape, the park is a beautiful setting nearly any time of year.

The visitors' center is only open Fridays, Saturdays, and Sundays, but it contains a wealth of information about both the park and its flora. The British Camp Trail leaves from the parking lot, looping around what is thought to have been the Musgroves' original property. During a summer visit, bird and cicada calls echo through the hardwood forest, which later opens up to an undeveloped field. The relatively flat trail skirts the picturesque Enoree River before turning back and passing a dammed pond dotted with picnic facilities. Despite being only one mile long, the trail passes through a variety of habitats as it heads back to the visitors' center. It passes through a hardwood forest with Eastern red cedar, beech, sourwood, river birch, black cherry, and osage orange. While osage orange, with its orange-colored bark, is not native to the area, it was widely planted as an ornamental tree in the 19th century. Its hardwood was valued for its fence building properties, and several large species can be seen in the park, specifically directly in front of the visitors' center. With open fields, woods, and flowing water, the park is also a good area for birding enthusiasts.

Eventually, the state hopes to build a bridge across the Enoree to link the two sides of the park, but for now visitors must drive 3.5 miles to Horseshoe Falls to explore the rest of the park. Many locals flock to this area on hot summer weekends,

This monument honors Mary Musgroves's reported colonial heroism during the Revolutionary War.

In 1780, about 400 Patriot and Loyalist soldiers clashed at Musgrove Mill, in a battle that was considered a turning point in the war.

tops of small ridges with gently sloping hillsides. Leaf-littered pathways guide you through a hardwood and loblolly pine forest resplendent with magnificent trumpet, cross, and muscadine vines that rival small trees in their stem diameter. Parts of the trail allow visitors to walk along what is believed to be the location of an old road used by settlers and soldiers in the 18th century. Informative signage details the historical significance of the park along the route and points out specific battle sites. In the springtime, the path showcases cranefly orchids, butterfly weed, spotted St. John's wort, smooth Solomon's seal, and spiderwort flowers.

Alternatively, visitors can bring their own watercraft and use a park system boat launch near Horseshoe Falls to paddle down the slow-moving Enoree River. Edward Musgrove chose this property for its location along the Enoree River, whose bouldered waters could provide power for a grist mill, enabling local farmers to grind grain without undertaking long journeys to more populated areas. He ran his plantation with enslaved labor, and the remnants of his home can still be seen at the park near the visitors' center. There are no mill remnants on the property.

When the Revolutionary War broke out, Musgrove believed himself too old to join the fighting. While he preferred to remain

not for its historical significance, but to enjoy the refreshing waterfall, including a handicapped-accessible shallow swimming hole located on Cedar Shoals Creek. Here, cool water takes a gentle plunge off 10-foot rock outcroppings that form the upper creek. Below the falls, the soft riverbed is a welcome respite for families that picnic along the stream's banks while children splash in the refreshing tonic.

The 1.3-mile Battlefield Trail takes off from this area, rising from the river bottom to neutral, his property was claimed by the British and their Loyalists, who utilized the home as a hospital and the mill as a source of food for their soldiers. The site was important for its proximity to roads linking the area to the rest of the state. By claiming important properties and roadways, the British sought to control transportation routes and move supplies throughout the region.

In August 1780, about 200 Patriots planned an attack on Loyalist troops. When the Patriots arrived, however, they were surprised to find the 200 Loyalists reinforced with another 300 British regulars. While attempting to spy on their enemies, American Patriots were detected. The 500-strong British force quickly assembled and set the stage for a battle against the outnumbered Patriot militiamen. Patriot troops, however, outwitted their rivals by luring them into an ambush in an open field that rendered them vulnerable to the surrounding Patriot troops. In the end, the bloody battle caused 137 British casualties, compared to only 16 American deaths. The Battle of Musgrove Mill was considered a turning point in South Carolina's participation in the Revolutionary War, coming on the heels of a devastating loss at Camden and propelling the Patriot militias toward their next important victory at Kings Mountain.

History buffs can enjoy occasional reenactments and living history festivals at Musgrove Mill, generally in mid-April. Otherwise, it is a good destination to wander around, take in some history, enjoy some beautiful scenery, and maybe even enjoy a nice swim at Horseshoe Falls.

GOOD TO KNOW

NEARBY ATTRACTIONS:
Cross Keys Plantation is a living history museum that features tours, reenactments, and demonstrations of life in the 1800s.

OPTIMAL TIME TO VISIT:
Year-round for hiking and learning about Musgrove Mill's role in the Revolutionary War. Wildflowers appear in the spring. Wade in or canoe the waters during the summer.

WHAT'S UNUSUAL:
Diverse plant life on two trails and Revolutionary War history.

BRING:
Water and a canoe.

OCONEE STATE PARK

624 State Park Road
Mountain Rest, SC 29664
Oconee County
southcarolinaparks.com/
oconee

OCONEE STATION STATE HISTORIC SITE

500 Oconee Station Road
Walhalla, SC 29691
Oconee County
southcarolinaparks.com/oconeestation

Oconee State Park and Oconee Station State Historic Site are nestled in the corner of the state where North Carolina, Georgia, and South Carolina meet and create a diverse topography that botanically supports numerous wildflowers and plants. Because this region is the site of severe drop-offs from the surrounding Piedmont mountains, visitors can spot large waterfalls and enjoy hikes along the parks' rolling hills.

TO DO: 🥾 ⛺ 🎣 🛶 🏊 🏠 🔭 📷 📖   **FEE: YES**

While the two parks are only four miles apart, it takes about 25 minutes to travel from one to the other by car. However, hikers can visit both by taking the Oconee Connector, a four-mile trail that drops 800 feet in elevation and connects the state park to the state historic site. The trek from Oconee State Park to Oconee Station State Historic Site is mostly downhill, whereas traversing the two destinations requires a fairly strenuous climb. Both parks have hiking trails, but Oconee State Park has more options.

One of the most popular destinations at the Oconee State Historic Site is the 70-foot Station Cove Falls, which can be accessed by an easy half-mile trail from the historic site's parking lot. The Oconee Connector Trail passes close to these falls as well, allowing for a quick visit when coming down from Oconee State Park. In the springtime this trail bursts with an unbelievable display of several varieties of trilliums and mayapple flowers. The flowers cover the ground as far as one can see in more than one area of the walk.

Also in Oconee Station are two historic buildings—a home and an 18th-century outpost for the South Carolina militia. Oconee Station was built on top of a hill to provide backcountry settlers with a place where they felt safe from Native Americans, and it later became a trading post. Throughout the year, the State Park System offers historical events at the park, including reenactments. Rangers are often on hand to interpret and provide more information on the area's historical significance. The lake at Oconee Station is stocked with largemouth bass and bluegill for fishing, and an easy one-mile hike will take visitors around the picturesque lake.

At Oconee State Park visitors can hike to Hidden Falls, a 50-foot waterfall, via a 2.5-mile trail that is a spur of the Foothills Trail. Another interesting excursion is the Lake Trail, a flat path that runs along the lakeshore and passes through a wetlands area. Here, bullfrogs can be heard bellowing, and visitors can view an old water wheel that has been relocated to this site. Explore the 1.5-mile Old Waterwheel Trail to see the stone edifice that previously housed this artifact. In addition, the 76-mile Foothills Trail starts in Oconee State Park and currently ends at Table Rock State Park, crossing back and forth across the South and North Carolina borders. There are plans to eventually continue the trail to the coast. Explore the state park website for a full list and description of the trails.

A historic water wheel pays homage to the commerce that once took place here.

The rare Oconee bells, which require a specialized habitat found in very few areas of the state, can be seen along the Oconee Trail in Oconee State Park where a wooden fence marks their location. For a few weeks in March, these waxy-leafed plants bloom with tiny white and yellow flowers. Oconee bells prefer moist, hilly areas, so the trail becomes a little steep where these unique plants grow. Equally rare is the chestnut tree, which can be seen along the Wormy Chestnut Trail. Chestnuts were largely eradicated in the South by the chestnut blight, and even to this day, they rarely live long before becoming infected.

During the Great Depression, the Civilian Conservation Corps (CCC) had a heavy hand in the development of the state's park system, and its influence is still evident. A giant bronze statue of a CCC worker sits underneath an American flag outside the visitors' center. The CCC built 19 rustic cabins at Oconee State Park, which have since been updated and are available to rent. Many of the cabins sit on the lake and feature hardwood floors, fireplaces, fire pits, picnic tables, a small kitchen, and either one or two bedrooms. The CCC additionally built the old water wheel structure, the water fountains,

Station Cove Falls is an easy half-mile hike from Oconee Station State Historic Site.

the bathhouse, and one of the picnic shelters.

Oconee State Park is technically part of a temperate rainforest. Moss and other lush groundcover plants are abundant in this park, which is a sea of green during the spring and summer. The plentiful rain also explains why frogs and salamanders love the park.

Because of its large size, Oconee State Park has many non-hiking related activities as well. The lake is stocked with both rainbow and brown trout, bream, and catfish. Visitors may bring their own gear or rent some from the visitors' center. Pedal boats also are available to rent. In the summer when the lake is open for swimming, it is one of the few places in the state where a high dive remains. (There is also a high dive at Table Rock State Park.) Children love jumping off the diving board as a lifeguard looks on. Another popular, family-friendly activity is the mini-golf course, which is the only course in the State Park System. Balls and clubs can be rented from the State Park office. In the summer months, local bands perform bluegrass music, and there is square dancing in the large, scenic barn on the property.

GOOD TO KNOW

NEARBY ATTRACTIONS:
Buzzard Roost Heritage Preserve, about 25 miles south, has a number of rare plant species, including the federally-endangered smooth coneflower. Birders enjoy the many warblers that visit.

Keowee Toxaway State Park (page 36)

Stumphouse Tunnel (page 64)

Apple picking is a fun fall activity in Mountain Rest, SC. Several orchards exist nearby.

OPTIMAL TIME TO VISIT:
In the spring to see the plethora of wildflowers at both Oconee Station and Oconee State Park, including the Oconee bell. In summer, the park provides many activities such as swimming, a high dive, pedal boats, and bluegrass music.

WHAT'S UNUSUAL:
A temperate rainforest, the beautiful Station Cove Falls, an unusual clump of chestnut trees, and the incredibly rare Oconee bells.

BRING:
Water.

PARIS MOUNTAIN STATE PARK

2401 State Park Road
Greenville, SC 29609
Greenville County
southcarolinaparks.com/parismountain

Amidst a swath of rolling hills and gently flowing streams, Paris Mountain suddenly explodes onto the landscape—an emblem of an ancient mountain range that has long since eroded away. The area is a favorite among Greenville residents for its numerous hiking and biking trails, clear-running streams, and cool respite from warm temperatures at lower elevations.

TO DO: 🥾 ⛺ 🎣 🛶 🏊 🔭 📷 📖 🚴 🏠   **FEE: YES**

Technically, Paris Mountain is a basalt monadnock, an isolated mountain that abruptly rises above the surrounding countryside. South Carolina's Piedmont region has several monadnocks, many of which have been set aside for public use. Perhaps due to both its location and the well-preserved nature of its land, Paris Mountain is one of the State Park System's most popular destinations, pulling in more than 400,000 visitors a year. Despite these numbers, the park seldomly feels crowded.

At its peak, Paris Mountain is 1,300 feet above the city of Greenville, a mere five miles away. This sudden elevation change creates great rolling trails and fosters a beautiful Piedmont forest that sparkles with color during autumn months.

Paris Mountain boasts an old-growth hardwood forest, the result of protective measures dating back to the 19th century. The resulting canopies, from white oaks, hickories, poplars, and sizeable chestnut oaks, shade summer hikers from infamous South Carolina heat, yet open up those same trails to sunshine during cooler winter months. Also worth noting are some of the park's interesting plants: Rosebay rhododendrons grow along some of the riverbanks and bloom in late spring into the early summer, and Virginia pine can be found in the highest areas of the park. Other plants normally found at the base of the Blue Ridge Mountains also grow here. Trailing arbutus, a perennial that bears small pink flowers, then red fruit, blooms in March and April along many trails, and wild violets that range from a pale blue to a deep purple are found in the park.

The Paris Mountain Water Company developed Paris Mountain, building several lakes and dams here between 1889 and 1918 in order to create Greenville's first water system. Later, water was tapped from other sources, and the city donated the land for use as a state park in 1935.

The water is a draw for summer visitors who like to take advantage of the 15-acre Lake Placid near the park's entrance. Lifeguards are on duty seasonally, and visitors may rent canoes and pedal boats from springtime through the early fall.

The 1,500-acre park is shaped like a panhandle, with a narrow strip of land at the entrance that opens up to the greater mountain area. The 16 miles of trails are well connected and well marked, and hikers can choose from a

The Civilian Conservation Corps constructed the original bridges, dams, and buildings throughout Paris Mountain State Park.

The accurately named Lake Placid is a favored place to swim or paddle during summer months.

variety of paths, many of which loop back to original parking areas. The visitors' center sells trail maps, and downloadable ones are available online for free prior to visiting the park.

Sulphur Springs is one of the prettiest hikes at the park but can be a bit strenuous with rocky paths and hilly areas. The 3.5-mile trail follows a quiet stream up the mountain, the sound of cascading water an apt accompaniment to the trampling of hiking boots. Along the way is a beautiful groundcover aptly named running pine. True to its name, this plant resembles a dense population of miniature trees covering the forest floor.

After less than a mile, hikers find what appears to be an old castle turret directly below the dam of Mountain Lake. The stone turret actually housed the dam valve for this small reservoir that once provided water to Greenville. During the 1890s, water was purified by traveling through the rocky substrate of Mountain Creek on

its journey to Greenville. Today, the streams are home to many insects that require clean water, such as stonefly, mayfly, dobson, and dragonfly nymphs. Crayfish and salamanders also can be found.

Continuing on, the path veers from the stream but connects with other trails that allow hikers to see an old fire tower, a larger lake, and beautiful views of the surrounding landscape. Dense vegetation in the spring and summer months often impedes visibility on these hikes, but a lack of foliage in the wintertime opens up great views of the forest, making this hike interesting year-round. Look for the evergreen holly bush that does not normally appear in this region of the state. Cranefly orchids are found in the springtime, evident by the absence of leaves until after the flower has finished blooming.

Brissy Ridge is a 2.5-mile trail that can be taken from the middle of the Sulphur Springs Trail and offers some of the best views in the park. It further connects to Kanuga Trail, leading to the park's largest 15-acre lake, referred to simply as Reservoir #3, which is open for fishing use only. The water in each of these former reservoirs is clean and beautiful, one of the reasons it was selected as Greenville's source of water. Today, fishermen can catch bream, bass, and crappie in the lakes.

There are about 15 miles of hiking trails, but sections of eight of the trails are joint hiking and mountain biking trails. The park offers an abundance of resources to biking enthusiasts, a rarity in the State Park System. Paris Mountain has been the site of a downhill mountain biking race in past years, and George Hincapie, a Tour de France participant and Greenville native, is said to have trained at the park. Trails are closed to bikes on Saturdays, however, and most bikers are respectful of hikers on other days.

Plants that can be found here include spotted wintergreen, downy rattlesnake plantain, bloodroot, and Carolina silverbell. The partridge berry that is common here is also known as twin flower for the dual set of flowers that are needed to produce a single red berry on this plant. The berry brightens the forest floor throughout the winter.

The park owes its name to an early settler named Richard Pearis who married a local Cherokee woman and became close to the Native Americans in the region. The park is one of 16 in the state that was developed by the Civilian Conservation Corps, a Depression-era work program. Still in use, although only partly renovated, is the old CCC bathhouse, which now serves as an interpretation center with impressive 3D maps, descriptions of plants found at the park, and taxidermy animals. The park also rents out Camp Buckhorn Lodge—a dining hall and meeting facility

with nine primitive cabins—for group use. Additionally, a CCC work crew replaced Lake Placid's original dam, which was constructed in 1898. Paris Mountain earned its spot on the National Register of Historic Places because of the multitude of CCC-built structures within its bounds. These structures beautifully complement the landscape, creating an alluring park that is close to one of South Carolina's nicest cities.

GOOD TO KNOW

NEARBY ATTRACTIONS:
Lake Conestee Nature Park has 400 acres and miles of trails along the Reedy River south of Greenville. Beaver, otters, salamanders, and many other animals live in the forests and wetlands of the park.

Falls Park in downtown Greenville offers beautiful waterfalls and a family-friendly park next to the Reedy River.

The 20-mile **Swamp Rabbit Trail** runs between Greenville and Travelers Rest and provides great views of the Reedy River throughout. Several orchards exist nearby.

OPTIMAL TIME TO VISIT:
In the fall to enjoy fall color; summer to swim and enjoy the slightly higher elevations.

WHAT'S UNUSUAL:
Sudden elevation changes for enjoyable hiking and mountain biking.

BRING:
Water and a bike.

STEVENS CREEK HERITAGE PRESERVE

State Road 33-88 near Highway 19
Clarks Hill, SC
McCormick County

While there is only a 1.3-mile loop trail that snakes through Stevens Creek Heritage Preserve, there may be no place in South Carolina that provides a more beautiful yield of springtime ephemerals. The preserve is a little off the beaten path, about 20 minutes north of Augusta, but it is well worth the travel time—just don't forget to pack the camera!

TO DO: 🥾 🔭 📷   **FEE: NO**

Sometimes finding heritage preserves is a bit challenging as they lack physical addresses. To visit Stevens Creek, take S.C. Highway 230 (exit 1) off I-20 and head north for 9.3 miles. Turn left on secondary road 143 and proceed eight miles, crossing the Stevens Creek bridge. The preserve's parking area is about one mile from the bridge. Directions are also listed on the website of the state's Department of Natural Resources (DNR).

A DNR kiosk in the parking lot introduces the preserve, providing maps and area information. From here, a short trek down the path unveils the loop path. Heading to the right will bring hikers first to the higher forested area of the preserve, where oaks and pines dominate, and then to the creek, where the spring ephemerals are most abundant. We recommend taking the upland trek first to build up excitement for the profusion of flowers that dominate the landscape at the end of the hike, but either direction is viable.

One of the most unusual plants found at Stevens Creek is the rare Miccosukee gooseberry, a variety found only at Florida's Lake Miccosukee and in the low-lying areas of Stevens Creek. The plant has small, green flowers dangling from its branches in March, bearing fruit in April and May. Oddly, new leaves do not accompany the flowers

in springtime but appear in the fall and during the winter months when the plant captures sunlight without competing with the deciduous trees around it. By mid-summer, it will discard its leaves. This is South Carolina's only native gooseberry, a thorny species that does not appear to bear fruit once transplanted and is difficult to germinate.

Another unusual flower is the false rue anemone, whose only known statewide location is also at Stevens Creek. This is a petite flower, bearing five white petals accompanied by bright yellow stamen. It is easy to confuse this flower with the windflower that also blooms along the creek, but the latter has seven white petals. The popular shooting star flower, a member of the primrose family, also blossoms profusely at Stevens Creek Heritage Preserve. As its name

In addition to a variety of wildflowers, morel mushrooms also are common at Stevens Creek Heritage Preserve.

GOOD TO KNOW

NEARBY ATTRACTIONS:
The **Aiken parks** are all approximately an hour from here (Hitchcock Woods, page 90; Aiken State Park, page 74).

OPTIMAL TIME TO VISIT:
In the spring—late March to mid-April—to see wildflowers in bloom.

WHAT'S UNUSUAL:
Soil with unusually high pH fosters 15 rare spring ephemerals along with a variety of other flowers.

BRING:
Water and a camera.

suggests, this white flower has petals that are thrown backwards, giving the impression that it is hurtling through space. Flower lovers adore this flower because of its size and beauty.

It is easy to recognize trilliums, another flower at the preserve, by the three large leaves that fan out atop their short stalks. The lance-leaf trillium is the rarest, sporting a garnet red flower that points up to the sky—a severe contrast to the three green and silver leaves that point downward. The pale yellow trillium is true to its name in color, and offers a scent reminiscent of cloves. Unlike the other trilliums found here, the southern nodding trillium hides its white or maroon flowers beneath its large leaves; hikers won't notice these blooms unless they look carefully.

Another flower found here but rare to our state is Dutchman's breeches. This little bloom resembles a small pair of pants hung out on a line to dry. It is more commonly found in states that are farther north. Other flowers in this preserve include spring beauty, trout lily, wild geraniums, hepatica, green violet, golden ragwort, and hairy spiderwort. Because of moist soil, alert hikers also will find a good many morel mushrooms growing alongside the path.

In the pine forest segment of the trail, flowers tend to appear more on bushes and trees. These include the dogwood, Carolina silverbell, and mock orange. It's a good idea to bring a flower book to help identify the great array of flowers found at this heritage preserve.

Stevens Creek is home to many rare flowers, likely because of its unusually calcium-rich soil. This area is thought to be a relic of a hardwood forest that existed in South Carolina during the last ice age about 12,000 years ago. In the late 1950s, University of North Carolina botany professor Albert Radford detailed finds of rare and as-yet-unknown plants at the site. Radford wrote a scientific paper, postulating the discovery of a "relic plant community." He attributed the continued existence of many of these rare plants to the presence of unusual soil that has a higher pH than most Carolina soil, but similar to the levels found in the Appalachian Mountains. His discovery led the state to purchase the property, with the help of the Nature Conservancy, and set it aside as a 434-acre heritage preserve.

In addition to the unusual plants, Stevens Creek also is home to the rare Webster's salamander. The best chance to see this mottled reddish-orange salamander is where the path crosses the small creek. Normally, however, this shy creature hides out below leaves and in rock crevices in stream beds.

Stevens Creek is a bit off the beaten path, but the unusual ecosystem found here definitely outweighs the travel time. This heritage preserve is known to harbor 15 rare plant species and the elusive Webster's salamander. Although it is a small place, hikers should give themselves a few hours to stroll the preserve and see all it has to offer.

Shooting stars (top) *can be found along streambeds in the spring. Strawberries* (below), *as well as blueberries and gooseberries, also are plentiful.*

STUMPHOUSE MOUNTAIN HERITAGE PRESERVE YELLOW BRANCH PICNIC AREA

Westbound from Walhalla off Highway 28
Mountain Rest, SC 29664
Oconee County
www.oconeecountry.com/stumphouse.html

Located in the corner of the state, Stumphouse Mountain Heritage Preserve houses the scenic Isaqueena Falls and is directly across the highway from the popular Yellow Branch Falls. These two tall cascades are prime examples of the marvelous waterfalls for which Oconee County is so well known. It is well worth an in-depth look at the 440 acres that make up this heritage preserve where beautiful rhododendrons, intriguing bat caves, and unique trails abound.

TO DO: 　　**FEE: YES**

Isaqueena Falls is located directly off a small parking area within the Stumphouse Mountain Preserve. It is easy to access the waterfall via a short wooden walkway with a platform that provides great views of its plunging water. Isaqueena Falls is named after a Cherokee woman who, legend has it, married a white man, much to the chagrin of her people. In order to escape their fury, it is said that she pretended to leap to her death from the waterfall while actually hiding beneath a rocky outcrop. Cherokees believe that evil spirits live around waterfalls and, thus, were hesitant to further investigate her leap. The beautiful name given to the falls is paralleled in its 100-foot drop, which can be seen either from the viewing platform or by an unauthorized steep path that leads to the base of the falls.

Across from the viewing platform is a yellow-blazed trail that explores the adjacent forested area. This roughly three-mile out-and-back trail is very flat as it was originally carved into the mountain for a railroad line that was halted due to the onset of the Civil War. The wide path is well marked and easy to navigate, and it crosses several interesting sites.

The beginning of this trail, known as the Boy Scout Trail, cuts through a large, rocky canyon as it makes its way towards several different access points of the incomplete railroad line. Large rocks surround the trail, making the hiker feel as if he or she is wandering through a rocky gorge or a deep ravine, even though the elevation remains steady.

The first section of the trail includes signs created during the completion of an Eagle Scout Service project through the Boy Scouts of America which identify the types of trees that grow along the path: hickories, oaks, and maples, to name a few. These trees border a wide path and create a thick, shady canopy. In the fall, trodden yellow and orange leaves cover the forest floor.

The first evidence of the incomplete railroad line comes approximately half a mile into the hike where visitors have the opportunity to climb into Middle Tunnel. Middle Tunnel is one of the never-completed access points for the railway. Railroad workers labored on the tunnel

Construction on Stumphouse Tunnel was halted during the Civil War and never resumed.

Isaqueena Falls is named for a Native American woman who according to legend leaped from the falls while being chased by her own people.

fungal disease known as white-nose syndrome. Bats are huge predators of mosquitoes and other insects, with some varieties eating as much as their own weight in insects nightly.

The path continues for another 2.2 miles before reaching the last tunnel and trail terminus. Water pools and drips in this section as sourwood trees, mountain laurel, holly trees, many varieties of ferns, and rhododendron spring up alongside it. In the spring, wildflowers such as trilliums, violets, anemone, and wild geraniums sprout up along the trail. Other beautiful plants in the preserve include sassafras trees, red cedars, and Carolina silver bell—a tree with alluring, white blossoms. Poison ivy runs rampant in the park, so visitors should use caution and be wary of this hairy vine that climbs many tree trunks.

in three different sections, which allowed many workers to dig simultaneously. To see this section of the tunnel, visitors must crawl into an underground hole that is ultimately obstructed from farther passage by a gate. This gate allows bats to come and go freely but prevents humans from entering the cavern.

Stumphouse Preserve is home to six different species of bats, including the rare Rafinesque's big-eared bat. Several bat species are in decline due to loss of habitat as well as a little-understood

The largest completed portion of Stumphouse Tunnel also is located within the preserve. A parking lot across from Isaqueena Falls marks the entrance to the tunnel. Signs near the parking lot explain the tunnel's historical significance to the area. The climb to the granite tunnel is steep, and an old railroad car sits outside its entrance. The inside is cool and moist, which makes entering the tunnel akin to stepping inside an overly air-conditioned room. This natural air conditioning makes Stumphouse Tunnel a great destination on those notoriously hot South Carolina days. Additionally, because of the cool temperature, Clemson University once utilized the tunnel to cure blue cheese—a process that requires the specific type of environment that Stumphouse provides.

Directly across the street from this preserve lies the Yellow Branch Picnic Area, where the Yellow Branch Trail leads to a possibly more impressive waterfall that cascades 50 feet down jagged rocks. Locals consider this waterfall one of the most picturesque in the state, and many have compared the rocks that make up the falls to stacked books. The grandeur and width of the waterfall only add to its splendor.

The hike to Yellow Branch Falls is a short and easy 1.5-mile out-and-back trail. Most of the trail is flat and crosses several streams with wooden bridges or evenly-placed flat stones along the way. Because the trail frequently touches a clear mountain stream, it is quite lovely. The path becomes very narrow as it nears the waterfall, wandering alongside a steep ridge. During the springtime, wildflowers bloom along the rocky ground near the waterfall, including mayapple and trillium.

It is rare to have two beautiful waterfalls as near to each other as Yellow Branch and Isaqueena Falls. Visitors should take the opportunity to see each of these falls and enjoy the rich history of Stumphouse Mountain Heritage Preserve.

GOOD TO KNOW

NEARBY ATTRACTIONS:
Whitewater Falls, approximately 30 minutes away, is directly across the North Carolina border and features a waterfall that drops roughly 400 feet down a rocky slope. The hike to these falls is short, yet there are numerous other hikes on the property.

Oconee Station State Historic Site (page 52)

OPTIMAL TIME TO VISIT:
In the fall to enjoy yellow and orange foliage or in the spring to see a variety of wildflowers.

WHAT'S UNUSUAL:
A series of tunnels that date back to before the Civil War; two large waterfalls so close together.

BRING:
Water.

TABLE ROCK STATE PARK

158 Ellison Lane
Pickens, SC 29671
Pickens County
southcarolinaparks.com/tablerock

Named for the iconic bald mountain top that rests within the park, Table Rock State Park is a haven of 3,000 acres just waiting for exploration. While the backdrop for the park is its most well-known attribute, the park also boasts two lakes (36-acre Lake Pinnacle and 67-acre Lake Oolenoy), six trails, and historic Depression-era structures.

TO DO: 🚶 ⛺ 🎣 🚣 🏊 🔭 📷 📖 🏠 **FEE: YES**

Table Rock State Park is most commonly associated with the steep hike that ascends the summit of its namesake. This popular hike, which is 3.6 miles one way, is a grueling uphill climb; however, standing atop the bald outcropping that makes Table Rock famous is well worth the sore muscles. From the granite peak, the views are outstanding: forests, hills, and reservoirs dot the floor below in an expanse of greens and blues (or yellows, oranges, and blues in autumn). The truly lucky also may spot a peregrine falcon or one of the many other raptors that frequent these hills.

The trail passes several quintessential landmarks along the way. Enormous granite boulders dot the trailside, surrounded by oak and hickory trees. In the spring and early summer, beautiful purple irises spring up alongside the path while native azaleas and dogwoods burst into bloom. Roughly halfway up the trail is a trailside shelter built by the Civilian Conservation Corps (CCC). This is a great place to relax and take in an incredible view of the surrounding Piedmont foothills. The trail also passes Governor's Rock, an expansive granite sheet, which provides another opportunity to take in the views. Along the way, listen for the brown-headed nuthatch that sounds incredibly similar to a squeaky bath toy, along with a variety of warblers, woodpeckers, and other birds that call Table Rock home.

For those looking for an easier hike, the park's 1.9-mile Lakeside Trail encompasses many of the special aspects of Table Rock State Park without delivering sore muscles. The trail ambles past Pinnacle Lake, CCC-constructed buildings, such as the Table Rock Lodge and spillway, and the famous Table Rock Mountain itself. Similarly, the Carrick Creek Trail is an easy two-mile loop that also highlights the park's incredible landscape. The trail meanders along Carrick Creek, offering views of small waterfalls along the way. In the summer, this creek is filled with swimmers seeking a reprieve from the hot Carolina sun, but a careful eye may also detect a variety of salamanders and even crayfish. South Carolina has about 27 species of salamanders that can often be found in the cool mountain streams, hiding under leaf litter or rocks. Spotted salamanders, black with white dots, frequent Table Rock streams, as do black-bellied and red salamanders. Enjoy watching these aquatic animals swim but refrain from handling them, as doing so can pass along diseases that reduce their numbers.

For the truly hardy, the Pinnacle Mountain Trail is arguably more difficult than the Table Rock Trail and also offers great views. This 4.2-mile trail

Look for fungi, insects, and birds on dead trees along the path: it's a sign of a healthy forest.

climbs to Bald Rock Overlook, a granite outcropping on Pinnacle Mountain that looks out over the South Carolina foothills. Mill Creek Falls is one of the destinations along this trail and has a beautiful 25-foot cascade. Before Mill Creek Falls, hikers pass by the 20-foot Spring Bluff Falls, which is often dry except following rainfall. Spring Bluff Falls is directly adjacent to the trail, and thus when it runs, it is an excellent spot to cool off from the steep hike. For those who want to shorten the trail, Mill Creek Pass connects to the Ridge Trail, which leads back down the mountain. However, in doing so, hikers would bypass both Bald Rock Overlook and the peak of Pinnacle Mountain—the highest mountain completely in South Carolina at 3,419 feet. (Sassafras Mountain, the state's highest mountain, is on the North Carolina/South Carolina border and dips into both states.) After reaching the top of Pinnacle Mountain (which has

View the many cascades along Carrick Creek when hiking along the trail that bears its moniker.

obstructed views), hikers should traverse the Ridge Trail to the Table Rock Trail to make their way back to the nature center.

These trails are all dominated by American beech, eastern hemlock, tulip poplars, and a variety of oak and hickory trees. Mountain laurel and rhododendrons are in bloom in the springtime along with a variety of wildflowers, from Jack-in-the-pulpits to wild violets and trilliums. In the warmer months, bears frequent the park but are almost as elusive as the foxes and bobcats that also live here. More common are raccoons and turkeys.

For those not seeking a hike, Table Rock State Park has a handful of other great activities. In the summer months, the swimming hole is open on Pinnacle Lake, and the cost of swimming is included with admission. The lake here contains two diving boards: one high dive and one low dive. A variety of boats also are available to rent through the state park; private boating is only permitted on Lake Oolenoy, not Lake Pinnacle. A small playground borders the park and is a great stop for small children. Picnic shelters dot the park as well, and fishing is permitted in both lakes.

With so many hiking opportunities, Table Rock is a great place for an overnight visit. The State Park System recently overhauled and renovated the 14 cabins within the park, nine of which were built by the CCC. The one- and two-bedroom cabins are rustic, yet cozy, with a truly mountainous feel, thanks to their floor-to-ceiling wood paneling, fireplaces, and wood furniture. Screened-in porches with rocking chairs, fire pits lined with chairs, and wooden swings also add character to the cabins. Campsites with electrical hookups are available, and for the more adventurous, the park provides backcountry sites on the far side of the visitors' center.

Other amenities in the park include a country store that provides such camping essentials as s'mores ingredients and firewood, a visitors' center with information about the park, and a nature center which features a few live reptiles and amphibians. Alongside the main road through the park is also a pull-off spot that has great views of Table Rock Mountain.

Across from the visitors' center is the newest addition to the park, Camp Oolenoy. Construction on the camp began in 1856, and it is now listed on the National Historic Register. Several of the camp buildings were built later with the help of the CCC. Girls' and boys' dormitories, an old house, and a wooden smokehouse are among the structures on the property. The buildings are beautifully rustic, and signage illuminates their history.

Hiking to the summit of Table Rock is an iconic rite of passage for South Carolinians. Surrounded by native plants, a profusion of granite boulders, and incredible views over the foothills, the hike provides scenery not available at other destinations. Hike to the top and see what all of the fuss is about, and afterwards, cool off in the park's waters.

GOOD TO KNOW

NEARBY ATTRACTIONS:
The **Mountain Bridge Wilderness Area** is home to **Caesars Head** (page 12) and **Jones Gap State** (page 32) as well as a number of other trails and preserves.

Eastatoe Creek Heritage Preserve (page 26)

OPTIMAL TIME TO VISIT:
During the summer to experience the rewarding hike to the top of Table Rock and afterwards, to cool off in the lake or stream.

WHAT'S UNUSUAL:
Hiking to the top of the Table Rock granite dome and visiting historic camp Oolenoy. Table Rock also contains the South Carolina's highest peak that is entirely within the state's borders.

BRING:
Water and a good pair of hiking boots.

MIDLANDS/SANDHILLS

Located between the Piedmont and coastal regions of the state, the Midlands area is often ignored by its more showy siblings. Hidden in this zone, however, are some remarkable natural areas that blend a variety of eco-habitats and support an interesting array of flora and fauna. Here you will find bold rivers, floodplains supporting plants that are adaptable to varying conditions, and longleaf pine forests that have otherwise been nearly erased from our landscape by the relentless logging of the 1800s. Enjoy a canoe ride down the longest free-flowing black river in North America at one of several state parks. A venture into these parks and preserves will be an incredibly rewarding experience.

AIKEN STATE PARK

1145 State Park Road
Windsor, SC 29856
Aiken County
southcarolinaparks.com/aiken

South Carolina is home to the longest free-flowing blackwater river in North America, and Aiken State Park provides the perfect opportunity to quietly paddle along a short stretch of this idyllic waterway. The park features natural swampy areas, four lakes, and several artesian wells—areas that are historically significant in that they were developed by a segregated African-American work group during the Great Depression.

TO DO: 🥾 ⛺ 🎣 🛶 🔭 🏊 📷 📖 🐎 🚴 **FEE: YES**

Aiken is nestled in the Sandhills region of the state, although the river gives the aura of a more coastal area, with its subtle draping of Spanish moss and a vine-laced canopy that sometimes encloses the riverbed. The Edisto River meanders an astonishing 250 miles through South Carolina and is regaled as the only major river that lies entirely within the state. It begins as a spring-fed stream in Edgefield and Saluda counties before draining into the Atlantic Ocean near Edisto Beach. While dedicated and experienced paddlers travel much of this river, Aiken State Park is a great place for even novice paddlers to try their hand at canoeing.

The canoe trail is 1.7 miles long, and canoes can be rented from the park office for a nominal fee. Park staff members are generally happy to transport paddlers to the launching point, providing life vests and oars so that visitors can enjoy a one-way trip down the quiet river. Transit time on the canoe trail generally runs from 1.5 to 3 hours, depending on paddling speed.

Don't be misled by the blackwater moniker: Edisto is a surprisingly clear and robust river. The water is stained by the tannins of cypress trees as well as organic material that decomposes in the river, creating a dark brew likened to coffee or tea. The dark water only adds to the feeling of paddling through a lowcountry swamp as one drifts down the river, and it additionally seems to better reflect the surrounding landscape's images. Cypress trees, tupelo trees, and resurrection fern are abundant here, as are songbirds. Alligators are said to exist in Aiken but are a very rare sight, although snakes may be found occasionally, as is the case in much of South Carolina.

Aiken is one of the original 16 state parks developed by the federally-funded Civilian Conservation Corps (CCC) during the Great Depression. At this time, single, unemployed young men were put to work turning newly acquired but undeveloped public property into South Carolina's state parks. Segregation was still firmly entrenched in America, however, and CCC companies were racially divided in South Carolina. Roughly one-third of the CCC companies in South Carolina were composed of African-American men, and one such unit developed Aiken State Park. Company 4470 toiled for three years to build a superintendent's residence, two picnic shelters, and three fishing cabins. They also created

Artesian wells built by African-American members of the CCC decorate the park.

the dams that form the park's three small lakes. Pictures of the men are on some of the signage at the park, and the buildings are still in use today.

GOOD TO KNOW

NEARBY ATTRACTIONS:
Gopher Tortoise Heritage Preserve, about 15 miles south, is home of the federally-endangered gopher tortoise that exists only in the Southeast. This also is considered the state's best preserve for viewing the keystone species of wiregrass that coexists with longleaf pines.

Hitchcock Woods in Aiken (page 90)

For more nearby places see "Nearby attractions" in the chapter on Hitchcock Woods.

OPTIMAL TIME TO VISIT:
Spring to canoe the blackwater river and hike the trails.

WHAT'S UNUSUAL:
A park built by an African-American segment of the CCC; artesian wells; canoeing a blackwater river.

BRING:
Bugspray, a bathing suit, and gear to enjoy the activities.

Unusual at the park are the artesian wells, constructed by the CCC, where drinkable fresh water bubbles out around the clock from one of the many underground springs in the area. These can be found at the aptly named Fishing Lake, the canoe launching dock, and the park cabins. The abundant underground springs also feed the park's lakes.

Aiken State Park has more than 1,000 acres, but few trails. The Jungle Nature Trail derives its name from the dense vegetation that encroaches upon it. The flat trail winds around through the interior of the park, exposing a dry pine and hardwood forest resplendent with large rhododendron bushes. Hikers will walk past holly, sweet bay magnolia, wax myrtles, and a variety of other plants that thrive in the sandy soils here. Bracken ferns cover the forest floor.

The hike also showcases the park's swampland area. An elevated boardwalk takes

The slow-moving Edisto River provides a pleasurable boating experience, even for the novice paddler.

hikers over this area, which is fed by more freshwater springs. Carnivorous yellow pitcher plants and other vegetation that enjoy wet feet can be found in this area.

Springtime hikes will reveal beautiful wildflowers, such as Jack-in-the pulpit, while autumn will highlight colorful sassafras and hickory trees that paint the forest with reds and yellows.

The park is home to a wide range of birds, from warblers and tanagers to woodpeckers and flycatchers, hinting at the abundance of mosquitos that also call Aiken home (Bring the bug spray!). The bright-yellow prothonotary warbler can often be found along the Edisto River during its migration through the state. Yellow-billed cuckoos often are heard near the river and wetlands.

Year-round, Aiken is an intriguing park to visit with its enticing trails and easily paddled scenic river. Bring the entire family along to explore this hidden gem in South Carolina's Sandhills.

CAROLINA SANDHILLS NATIONAL WILDLIFE REFUGE

23734 Highway 1
McBee, SC 29101
Chesterfield County
fws.gov/refuge/Carolina_Sandhills

To stroll through the forests of Carolina Sandhills National Wildlife Refuge is to take a step back in time, observing plants and animals in abundance that are currently listed as endangered both locally and nationally. Two hundred years ago, when Europeans first arrived, approximately 90 million acres of longleaf pine flourished from Virginia to Texas. Today, less than three percent remains, and the wildlife dependent on this ecosystem is also in decline. The refuge offers the patient visitor an opportunity to see these unusual fauna and flora, although it helps to know what to look for.

TO DO: 🚶 🎣 👓 📷 🚴   **FEE: YES**

For starters, directly across from the visitors' center, a red-cockaded woodpecker (RCW) clan inhabits stately longleaf pines—the only tree suitable for this endangered bird. The RCW is a small woodpecker, about seven inches in length. It has a black and white barred back with a white neck and chest, and the male sports a small "cockade" of red feathers behind its eyes, though this is generally very difficult to observe with the naked eye.

These family-oriented woodpeckers spend years carving out cavities in dense, live longleaf pine trunks before establishing a hollow suitable for nesting. The hardwood pine tree forms a sticky sap when penetrated, thus preventing snakes and squirrels from readily invading nests. The flowing sap, common on RCW nesting trees, creates a "candle" effect that easily distinguishes the trees as woodpecker havens. Additionally, refuge staff members paint a thick, white strip around the base of the trees that have old or new cavities. The woodpeckers can be best viewed from April to July in the early morning hours when they are tending to nests and baby birds. There are about 125 RCW clans at the refuge—more than at any other refuge nationwide—so bring a pair of binoculars for an ideal opportunity to see this rare bird.

Before leaving the area, take in the longleaf pine ecosystem. Notably missing are the scrub brush and bushes prevalent in other pine forests. The longleaf pine requires frequent, low-intensity fires to thrive. The fires clear the ground of brush and needles so that seeds, dropping from cones in the autumn, can quickly sprout and find sunlight. Accompanying the pine are wiregrass and other fire-tolerant plants.

Yellow pitcher plants dominate the seepage bogs around Oxpen Lake at this wildlife refuge.

The elusive eastern fox squirrel also makes its home here. This incredibly large squirrel can measure up to two feet in length and weigh three pounds. Thus, it is sometimes mistaken for a fox. The fox squirrel spends most of its time on the ground, foraging for fruits and nuts, including the nuts from the longleaf pine. Both the fox squirrel and the flying squirrel have been known to appropriate a RCW's cavity for their lodging. Additionally, the refuge is home to beaver, extensive wild turkey populations, bald eagles, otter, fox, bobcat, and a host of other mammals.

The Carolina Sandhills Refuge offers

The purple pitcher plant shows off colorful blooms in early summer.

miles and miles of roads and trails in its almost 48,000 acres. It's a good idea to grab a map from the visitors' center before heading out in the car. Visitors Drive is a nine-mile long scenic road that winds through longleaf pine habitats, along some of the 30 lakes and ponds and beside open fields where visitors can often spot wild turkey. Along the way, there are a variety of trails up to 3.5 miles in length.

If visiting in early summer, the refuge has a spectacular show of blooming pitcher plants—an impressive, large carnivorous plant with beautiful flowers. A seepage area on the north side of Oxpen Lake offers one of the best displays of these unique plants with the hillside set aflame in intense yellows. Hikers are welcome to wander among the flowers, viewing the crafty pitcher tube that lures insects with nectar-secreting glands then traps them for additional protein. This area is also home to the endangered Pine Barrens treefrog, but its call is mostly heard at night: a rapid, nasally "quonk quonk" that is repeated at an impressive rate of about 25 times in 20 seconds. It tends to call for a mate on June evenings.

Another carnivorous plant in the refuge is the petite bladderwort, measuring only a few inches in size. The bladderwort flowers act as vacuums, sucking in prey along with water, and are plentiful at the Oxpen Lake viewing platform. The carnivorous sundew, which has sticky, star-like flowers, also can be found around this seepage area. The Oxpen area now has an observation tower, providing a panoramic view of the lake and surrounding fields. On a good day, white-tailed deer, turkey, hawks, waterfowl, and small mammals may be spotted. Fishing with a license is permitted at the lake.

The Lake Bee area has both picnic tables and restrooms. It is popular with birders, and a large number of species have been documented at the refuge, including the threatened Swainson's warbler. Some pitcher plants also are found in this area.

The open fields that are maintained at the refuge are the final habitat worth noting. These fields are planted as food crops for waterfowl, quail, dove, turkey, and deer. Pay them a visit to observe birds that prefer open areas: turkey, Mississippi kites, and bluebirds. These fields provide excellent wildlife habitat for the bobwhite, American kestrel, eastern kingbird, loggerhead shrike, eastern bluebird, blue grosbeak, indigo bunting, orchard oriole, and many other birds.

All together, 190 species of birds, 42 species of mammals, 41 species of reptiles, and 25 species of amphibians have been documented at the refuge.

The Carolina Sandhills National Wildlife Refuge was established in 1939. It is open year-round. The spring through autumn months are the best for viewing migrating birds. August, however, is a good time to view many wildflowers. Arrive early for your visit, and you will be amply rewarded with wildlife and intriguing plants.

GOOD TO KNOW

NEARBY ATTRACTIONS:
Sandhills State Forest, about 20 miles south, has wildflowers, pitcher plants, and longleaf pine forests. Some plants more typical of the Piedmont zone grow here.

Cheraw State Park (page 82)

OPTIMAL TIME TO VISIT:
Early summer to see endangered red-cockaded woodpeckers. In May to see large displays of yellow pitcher plants.

WHAT'S UNUSUAL:
The abundance of plants and animals oriented to a longleaf pine forest, including endangered species. The refuge also attracts 190 different bird species.

BRING:
Bug spray, water, binoculars, and a camera.

CHERAW STATE PARK

100 State Park Road
Cheraw, SC 29520
Chesterfield County
southcarolinaparks.com/cheraw

A splattering of bright yellow pitcher plants breaks up the thick carpet of native blue flag irises lining the headwaters of Lake Juniper in Cheraw State Park. The colors are vibrant among the shadows of Atlantic white cedars that send shafts of sunlight filtering through the tree canopy. This revered cypress swamp is afire with flowers in the spring and accessible either from a 4.5-mile hike through pristine forests or by canoes that float slowly over a meandering river. Either way, it is worth journeying to the northern edge of South Carolina to take in the sites of Cheraw State Park.

TO DO: 🥾 ⛺ 🎣 🛶 🏊 🔭 📷 📖 🏇 🚴 🏠 **FEE: YES**

Cheraw is South Carolina's oldest state park and was developed with the help of the Civilian Conservation Corps (CCC) in 1930. It is named after the Cheraw Indians who lived in the Piedmont areas of North and South Carolina, where this park is located. While these Native Americans no longer inhabit the area, the topography has remained the same—a stately and rare longleaf pine forest with accompanying wildlife and a verdant swamp.

When Europeans first arrived in the New World, longleaf pines dominated the landscape throughout the Southeast. However, these trees were heavily logged due to the demand for both their lumber and the turpentine created from their sap. A mere three percent of the longleaf pines that once thrived in the Southeast remains, and thus a variety of plants and animals dependent on this ecosystem struggle for their existence. Since Cheraw is one of the few longleaf pine forests in the region, the rare plants and animals that require this ecosystem thrive here.

Cheraw manages its 7,000-acre longleaf forest, meaning that rangers periodically burn the landscape as would happen naturally. If these forests do not experience fire, the landscape becomes severely altered and no longer supports its natural plants.

A 4.5-mile path allows visitors to see this extraordinary forest. Longleaf pine forests can foster up to 900 documented plant species that are found nowhere else in the world. Many researchers even maintain that this ecosystem is more diverse than the Amazon rainforest. It is home to nearly 30 federally endangered or threatened species, such as the red-cockaded woodpecker, golden heather, and pixie moss. The endangered Pine Barrens tree frog also lives close to the river that runs through the park and, despite its small size, sounds similar to a honking goose.

Using color and scent, the yellow pitcher plant lures insects inside its tube, trapping and ingesting them.

Since most longleaf pine forests were decimated, forests like Cheraw's are the result of plantings. Reestablishing longleaf forests is no easy task. These hardwood pines take up to 150 years to reach their full height of about 100 feet and can live more than 500 years. They are extremely fire resistant, and new seedlings do not emerge until after a fire has swept the land, creating open areas that nurture new trees. These forests also are home to a variety of sedges, grasses, carnivorous plants, and orchids.

Additionally, visitors should look for trees marked with painted white rings that denote red-cockaded woodpecker

GOOD TO KNOW

NEARBY ATTRACTIONS:
Carolina Sandhills National Wildlife Refuge (page 78)

Sandhills State Forest (page 81)

OPTIMAL TIME TO VISIT:
March and April when wildflowers are at their peak.

WHAT'S UNUSUAL:
The longleaf pine forests that dominate the park are home to many endangered species; a river that blooms with blue flag irises and yellow pitcher plants in the spring.

BRING:
Water, a camera, and bug spray

homes. The RCW, as it is called, exclusively nests in longleaf pines, and it is the only woodpecker that does not utilize dead snags to create nests. It takes between 100 and 200 acres to support one family cluster, which often includes one female and a dozen male birds. These woodpeckers perforate the bark near their nest cavities to encourage a trickling of sap that repels snakes and squirrels, giving the trees a dripping candle-like appearance. Older cavities may harbor flying squirrels, a nocturnal animal whose large eyes often can be seen peering out at visitors in the daytime. Also worth looking for are fox squirrels. These unusual animals are about twice the size of their gray squirrel cousins, averaging about two feet long. They are commonly dark gray, but are sometimes black, and they have a black facial mask with white patches on the nose, paws, and ears.

Conversely, visitors may enjoy the park by paddling a canoe around the 300-acre Lake Juniper and along the slow-moving river that feeds it. Rent canoes cheaply though the park office to see the dense cypress forest punctuated with cedars, wax myrtles, and other plants. Especially inviting, particularly to flies and other insects, are the bright yellow sweet pitcher plants, one of the many carnivorous plants found in this area. The yellow flower droops serenely over a tall funnel that lures insects down into sticky sap. These flowers bloom in dense clumps through the waterway in April and May. Several months during the year, the park also hosts a moonlight paddle, done usually near or at full moon. Call the park office or visit its website to check on scheduling and availability.

In late spring, blue flag irises illuminate the river, creating a carpet of periwinkle. Generally, the best time to view this stunning show is in April when pitcher plants also reveal their colors.

The spot where the river meets the lake gives paddlers a great view of several massive osprey nests. Osprey, like many other raptors, continue to utilize the same nest year after year, adding to it until it grows between three and six feet in diameter and up to 10 feet deep. During the spring, monogamous adult osprey can be seen catching and carrying fish back to these nests for hungry fledglings to devour.

Other worthwhile sights at the park include several original Civilian Conservation Corps buildings, an elevated boardwalk that takes visitors around the lake, and the much-touted 18-hole, par 72 golf course. The golf course has earned honors from the Audubon Society for a layout that preserves essential forest, and accolades from *Golf Digest* for being one of the best public courses in the nation. Tom Jackson designed the course, which was added in 1992.

Green fees remain quite reasonable at under $25 on weekends with cart fees at less than $20.

Cheraw is quietly situated near the North Carolina border, waiting to be appreciated for all that it protects. It offers the rare opportunity to hike in a well-maintained longleaf pine forest, or to boat along a stream teeming with carnivorous pitcher plants and blue flag irises. Consider staying at the park in one of eight CCC-built cabins that comfortably sleep four. Rent these cabins either daily or by the week. There are also 17 campsites, one of which is accessible only by water. Camping or lodging is a great way to experience Cheraw over multiple days, and thus really experience all that it has.

Prothonotary warblers frequent the headwaters of Lake Juniper.

GOODALE STATE PARK

650 Park Road
Camden, SC 29020
Kershaw County
southcarolinaparks.com/goodale

The expansive sky—a pale blue that stretches forever above the flat Sandhills of South Carolina—complements the tranquility of Goodale State Park's lake where the wide buttresses of large cypress trees rise up amongst reflective blackwater sprinkled with flowering waterlilies. American alligators skulk among the trees, while black anhingas perch on stumps to dry their wet feathers.

TO DO: 🚶 🎣 🛶 👓 📷   **FEE:** YES

Goodale State Park (pronounced "Good-all" by the locals) is a small park, a mere 763 acres, just outside of Camden. Perhaps due to its size, it is not one of the more popular state parks, being visited most often by nearby residents. However, a unique canoe trail paired with interesting water plants and great bird diversity makes this an essential trip for the South Carolina traveler.

The park's centerpiece is the Civil War-era millpond, a body of water ringed with tall pond cypress trees that harbors bream, bass, and catfish. In addition to fishing, this 140-acre lake provides great canoeing opportunities. The park office rents both fishing boats and canoes. A three-mile trail is fairly well-marked and guides visitors through a dense swamp environment. Another option is to simply meander alongside the lakeshore, away from the path, to get a chance to see the herons, killdeer, ducks, anhingas, and purple martins that frequent this area.

Before pushing off on the boat trip, however, take a minute to examine the plants on the lake's shore. Goodale State Park is home to several carnivorous plants that ingest insects to supplement the nourishment provided by the poor mineral content of Sandhills soil. The sweet pitcher plant is the most obvious, a 12-inch tall plant that sports red-streaked cylinders. Look closely to see the short, downward-facing hairs

that cause insects to become trapped deeper inside its channels. Nectar-secreting glands are the bait, and few insects return to the outside of the pitcher plant once lured down. A helpful flared leaf at the top of the funnel keeps rainwater from filling the basin. In the springtime, bright yellow flowers blossom from atop the plant.

It's easy to miss sundews because of their small size, but these carnivorous plants are just as bright and intriguing as the other carnivorous plants found at Goodale.

Another smaller but equally interesting carnivorous plant is the dwarf sundew, only a few inches tall but worth searching for near the boat ramp. The leaves on this plant, which capture various insects, resemble miniscule, sticky hair brushes. The plant's sweet secretions attract small prey that, once entrapped, usually die of exhaustion or asphyxiation. The plant then digests the insects through another set of secretions, converting them into a healthy protein.

On the canoe trail, be on the lookout for other fascinating plants that are generally associated more with waterways closer to the coast. The "Never Wet," or golden club, blooms in early spring with a tall spindle covered in small white flowers at its base and yellow ones nearer the tip. It earns its

Water is the centerpiece of this 763-acre park. There is plenty of great fishing.

name from its ability to repel water in beads. Several species of water lilies, floating hearts, and other aquatic plants are equally abundant.

Of course, you won't get far on the canoe trail without becoming aware of the many birds that utilize this habitat. Yellow-billed cuckoos, summer tanagers, blue-gray gnatcatchers, and vireos are just some of the birds commonly seen or heard on the trail. A favorite of birders is the prothonotary warbler, a canary-yellow bird that delights in darting through the swampy areas. The park places wood duck boxes strategically throughout the lake to attract these colorful ducks. In early spring, you often can observe ducklings plunging from their nesting boxes into the lake.

The canoe trail leads through a pond cypress forest. In Greek mythology, cypress is associated with Hades, the god of the underworld, and it doesn't take long for the dark waters of Goodale State Park to evoke sinister images. The plethora of flowers and abundance of songbirds, however, will quickly dissipate any feelings of uneasiness.

The park is home to several alligators, the largest being a 13-footer known locally as Elvis. (Elvis is quite large in girth, and locals named him to mock the singer's weight gain in later years.) However, chances of encountering these reptiles are slim; they are fairly reclusive and tend to stay away from visitors either on land or in boats. More worrisome is the surprisingly large number of red wasp nests hidden among shrubs on the canoe trail during late summer and early fall. These insects generally do not bother visitors unless their papery nests are smacked by an errant oar, so boaters should attempt to steer clear of all vegetation on the trail. The State Park System attempts to keep the nests under control and routinely patrols the canoe trail to make sure that these insects are not too prolific.

The canoe trail can take up to three hours if paddling at a leisurely pace. Look for diamond-shaped markers along the trail. It is not a loop, and there is no specific terminus, so paddlers can turn around as they tire or when the trail becomes too narrow to traverse further.

After returning to the boat landing, an inviting hike is the 1.5-mile Big Pine Tree Nature Trail loop that leads through a forest of pines, dogwoods, tulip poplars, eastern red cedars, and oak trees. Markers help visitors identify many plants, through which a variety of birds flit in and out. Another short path leads around part of the lake along the dam side. Here water gushes from the dam to form a small river in which salamanders and crayfish live.

The park has been open since 1955. It was named after N.R. Goodale, a Camden forester who led the local effort for Kershaw County to acquire the park. The county, in turn, conveyed it to the state in 1973.

To the locals, Goodale is a great place to picnic or fish on a quiet afternoon. Others will appreciate the cypress pond that is reminiscent of the coastal floodplains with its unusual carnivorous and water plants. Hunt for the blue heron rookery along the canoe trail for a chance to see the chicks in April or May. Goodale hosts a variety of treasures for those who take the time to look.

GOOD TO KNOW

NEARBY ATTRACTIONS:

Savage Bay Heritage Preserve is located on Drakeford Road near the town of Cassett. It is an undisturbed Carolina Bay that features pond cypress, broomsedge, and pines. It floods during wet periods but can also be completely dry at other times.

The **Camden Revolutionary War Site** features historic buildings and signage that discusses battles fought in this area. The site hosts Revolutionary War reenactments in the fall.

OPTIMAL TIME TO VISIT:

Spring and fall to experience the canoe trail at a temperate time.

WHAT'S UNUSUAL:

A Civil War era millpond that is the gateway to a canoe trail. Carnivorous plants that grow along the lakeshore.

BRING:

Water and a fishing rod.

HITCHCOCK WOODS

1700 Dibble Road
Aiken, SC 29802
Aiken County
hitchcockwoods.org

Hitchcock Woods owes its existence to the city of Aiken's strong equine roots, but the expansive 2,100-acre property is equally alluring to non-riders who will thrill at the varied topography and habitats. The park features unusual geological formations as well as plants that range from Spanish moss, typical of the coastal zone, to azalea and mountain laurels, which normally thrive in the Piedmont region.

TO DO:    **FEE: NO**

During the 19th century, Aiken was heralded as a winter respite for wealthy, horse-loving families. Thomas Hitchcock, a New York native who owned racehorses, was lured to the area by his wife, also a passionate equestrian. The sandy soils were considered optimal for training horses, and Hitchcock built a steeple track and other training facilities that are still in use today. He is also credited with introducing polo to the United States and originating the oldest fox drag hunt in the states.

In 1939, after his wife's death, Hitchcock set up a non-profit and donated 1,200 acres to the newly-created Hitchcock Woods Foundation. More property has been added over the years, and today there are about 70 miles of trails for both human and equine usage. Hitchcock Woods is considered the largest urban forest in America.

With seven entrances into the park, it is impossible to see all that Hitchcock Woods has to offer in a single day, but there are definitely several enticing options. The park provides free maps at all entrances, which are also downloadable from Hitchcock Woods' website. All paths are for pedestrians or horses only—bikes and motorized travel are forbidden. Dogs are permitted but, like people, they must cede the right of way to horses.

For first-timers, a good place to begin is at Fulmer Stables, located at 2180 Dibble Road. From this entrance, the picturesque Cathedral Aisle greets visitors. This dirt path gets its name from the trees that line it, forming a canopy that resembles the ribs of a gothic cathedral. This path is the first rail-to-trail project in the country. It uses the route where the South Carolina Railroad and Canal Company laid tracks in 1835 linking Charleston to Hamburg, a 136-mile stretch that helped farmers transport agricultural products, such as cotton, to the coast. The raised trail offers beautiful, albeit slightly obscured, views into adjacent wetlands. In addition, this scenic one-mile path leads to a spider web of other trails.

Another interesting trail is Peek-A-Boo Lane, which skirts the edge of impenetrable wetlands. Along this route, it is possible to view several of the six fern species known to exist in the woods: bracken, resurrection, cinnamon, ebony spleenwort, royal, and netted chain fern.

Of geological interest at Hitchcock are the Chalk Cliffs that are about one-half mile from Cathedral Aisle's terminus. An uphill jaunt unveils formations created by the presence of a hard kaolin dome that rises out of the sandy soil (technically referred

Longleaf pines grow throughout Hitchcock Woods.

to as a *vaucluse udorthent*). These 12-foot cliffs are a result of decomposed and compacted salt marshes that once existed in this area of the Midlands. The area has its own micro-environment featuring longleaf and Virginia pines growing naturally side-by-side, an unusual occurrence. Normally, Virginia pine does not grow so far south, although the area surrounding Aiken appears to have several disjunct populations.

Another excursion into the woods begins at 430 South Boundary Avenue where Hitchcock Woods' offices are located. At this entrance, hikers can view Memorial Gate, built in 1926 and dedicated to Thomas's brother, Francis. The area hosts the annual "Blessing of the Hounds" every Thanksgiving Day, a century-old event listed by the Huffington Post (2010) as one of "Ten Terrific Thanksgiving Traditions" throughout the country.

The Blessing of the Hounds marks the beginning of foxhunting season by spiritually blessing the animals for a safe and prosperous hunting season. Following the blessing, hounds and riders participate in a "drag hunt," a phantom foxhunt created by first dragging

Wildflowers, such as the aptly-named butterfly weed, are found throughout the park.

rags soaked in chemicals that mimic the odor of fox urine through the forest for the hounds to follow. The blessing has been held annually in Aiken since 1914. Hitchcock Woods is closed for fox hunting every Tuesday afternoon and Saturday morning from October through March. The Woods' official literature lists both red and grey foxes as area residents—hard to imagine given the frequency of hounds running noisily through its forests!

The Devil's Backbone Trail offers several views of Sand River, a dry, sandy creek bed that fills during heavy rainstorms, but whose water quickly permeates the soil, leaving only an empty, sandy ravine. There are several areas that seem to retain water a little longer than others, leading locals to warn of quicksand. There are a few mythical stories about this river, most notably the tale of a Native American chief who was led to this dry riverbed in search of a cure for his ailing daughter. Many still regard Sand River as a place of healing and well-being.

While the creek bed is fairly low in elevation, it is possible to climb a half of a mile up to Kalmia Trail where mountain laurel suddenly dominates the landscape. Aiken is technically located in the Sandhills region of the state but borders closely on the Piedmont zone, allowing for some overlap and introduction of unusual species such as mountain laurel, usually found at higher elevations. In the late spring, blossoms line the trail in a showy display. Ground juniper is a low-lying shrub normally found in the Appalachians and further north, but is also found in this area.

An intriguing juxtaposition is the Low Country Ride path in the southeast corner of Hitchcock Woods, best accessible from the 1120 Clark Road entrance to the park. The Low Country Ride is a hilly trail that dips low into the countryside where suddenly Spanish moss hangs heavily from trees and bushes. Springtime ephemerals are also notable here.

The Hitchcock Woods Foundation manages its property through controlled burns that encourage a longleaf pine forest ecosystem, with trail maintenance, and by attempting to control invasive species that proliferate in the park. The foundation recently agreed to participate in the national Safe Harbor program that rewards landowners for conservation efforts. The program encourages landowners to engage in conservation efforts that provide habitats for a variety of animals. Eventually, they hope to reintroduce the federally endangered red-cockaded woodpecker to the area. The foundation would like to have up to 10 red-cockaded woodpecker colonies in the woods and is working hard to manage the longleaf pine forest that will support them.

Hitchcock Woods is a must-see destination that celebrates Aiken's rich equine heritage as well as the area's unique habitats. Strap on a pair of hiking boots and come prepared to do some walking to take in the variety of landscapes that unfold in these woods. It is a Southern landscape at its best.

GOOD TO KNOW

NEARBY ATTRACTIONS:
Hopeland Garden, about two miles away, is a 14-acre formal garden accented by 100-year-old oaks within the city of Aiken. It includes wetlands, multiple fountains, and reflection pond.

Aiken State Park (page 74)

Gopher Tortoise Heritage Preserve (page 76)

OPTIMAL TIME TO VISIT:
Year-round for hiking, although summer heat can be daunting. Wildflowers appear in the early spring.

WHAT'S UNUSUAL:
A "river of sand" that flows only following heavy rains, a hillside Spanish moss trail, and mountain laurel and azalea displays, which are usually found in the Piedmont region.

BRING:
A horse and water.

COASTAL PLAIN/COASTAL ZONE

South Carolina's Coastal Plain extends from the Midlands to the sun-kissed coastal beaches, an area that was submerged below the Atlantic Ocean before waters receded 500 million years ago. It is a relatively flat area with a variety of unique habitats that support unusual plants and animals, from Venus fly-traps to roseate spoonbills. Birders flock to the Coastal Zone to see rare migrating birds that visit the state seasonally, while families are drawn to beaches where megalodon shark teeth are sometimes found. While humans have shaped the area greatly, preservationists have worked hard to restore and maintain its various habitats for generations to come.

BEAR ISLAND AND DONNELLEY WILDLIFE MANAGEMENT AREAS

585 Donnelley Drive
Green Pond, SC 29446
Colleton County
acebasin.net

The ACE Basin is named for the Ashepoo, Combahee, and Edisto rivers that snake serenely through the lowcountry until they dip their toes into the quiet solitude of the St. Helena Sound, eventually mingling with the salty water of the Atlantic Ocean. Flowing alongside acres of historic plantation homes, agricultural fields, cypress swamps, and tidal marshes, these rivers pass through a multitude of diverse habitats that are renowned for their beauty as well as the accompanying wildlife. The ACE Basin is composed of more than one million acres, making it one of the largest safeguarded estuarine systems on the East Coast.

TO DO: 🥾 🎣 🛶 🔭 📷 🚴 **FEE: NO**

While its size can be daunting, one of the best places to begin a visit to this ecological wonderland is via the Donnelley and Bear Island Wildlife Management Areas, located nearly adjacent to each other within the Ernest F. Hollings ACE Basin National Wildlife Refuge. These reserves, open daily to the public, are managed by the state Department of Natural Resources and are popular for hiking, biking, fishing, and hunting; but, for birding enthusiasts, it is the variety of avian species that is paramount.

Donnelley is an 8,000-acre property that was established in 1992. Where plantations and rice fields once flourished, an assortment of habitats are now managed, including forested wetlands, tidal marshes, agricultural fields, and some upland areas. It is home to many birds, including the federally threatened wood stork, the only stork native to the United States. During the winter months, the ACE basin provides an opportunity to see sandhill cranes, tundra swans, northern shovelers, gadwalls, and other varieties of ducks. Due to both the volume and diversity of birds that visit this property, the Audubon Society has listed it as an Important Bird Area in South Carolina.

Donnelley is accessible through several hiking and walking trails. It has two designated nature trails as well as miles of dirt roads accessible to foot and bicycle traffic. The Boynton Nature Trail is a three-mile loop that traverses through a maritime forest, former rice field dikes, and along smaller wetland areas. During spring and early summer months, it is not unusual to spot alligators, feral hogs, wood ducks, snakes, and bald eagles on this route. By late summer, droughts and excessive heat can make such sightings more sporadic.

The nearby Bear Island, likewise, has an assortment of habitats also conducive to migrating waterfowl. It boasts large expanses of marshes in addition to a forest and old rice fields. These wetlands will attract white pelicans, ducks, and other migrating waterfowl in the winter and songbirds in the spring and fall. At any time of year, bring along the binoculars for a chance to see all these birds.

The former rice fields are a key attractant to these birds as they contain a dike system fed by trunks, which allows water levels to be carefully maintained. A gradual drawdown of water concentrates populations of fish, crustaceans, gastropods, and insects that are the primary diet of wading birds.

Fox squirrels often are mistaken for raccoons, due to their large size and unusual facial markings.

Gulls, kingfishers, grebes, and ducks also utilize these impoundments.

As with many of the South's conserved properties, Donnelley and Bear Island management areas owe their existence to both hunters and the oft-maligned Yankees. In the 1700s, this was an area of antebellum mansions and expansive farms worked by African slaves. During the Civil War, most of South Carolina was decimated by Northern troops who burned many plantations to the ground. Farmlands fell out of use and became overgrown as their owners lacked both the resources to repair destroyed homes and the slave labor that made rice crops profitable. Northerners with a fondness for hunting bought up acreage, further fostering undeveloped areas to attract wildlife. While this was intrusive and unwelcome to many Southerners, it did, nonetheless, prevent further development of these lands.

As time passed and many bird populations were decimated, these hunters became increasingly respectful of the land and wildlife, and they have been on the forefront of conservation efforts by providing much-needed habitats. Conversions of rice fields to wildlife management areas provided habitats for migrating waterfowl. Today, hunters and conservationists are bonded in their desire to protect and preserve wetlands and other important habitats that allow animals to proliferate. The coastal areas have subsequently become bird migrating hotspots.

In 1988, the ACE Basin Project was created when a group of concerned citizens banded together to further protect the area from industrial and resort development. The preservationists joined forces with Ducks Unlimited, the Nature Conservancy, the South Carolina Department of Natural Resources, the U.S. Fish and Wildlife Service, and private landowners to create the ACE Basin Project. The uniform goal was to retain traditional usage of the land, allowing farming, forestry, recreation, hunting, and fishing to flourish. To this day, it is considered a highly unusual marriage of

Managed wetlands help lure migratory waterfowl to this area, from tundra swans to sandhill cranes.

government agencies, nonprofits, and private landowners that has worked together to preserve important habitats. Areas that are included in the ACE Basin include Bear and Donnelley Wildlife Management Areas, Edisto Beach State Park (page 116), Hunting Island (page 124), and Caw Caw Interpretive Center (page 108), among others.

The Ace Basin continues to expand as additional private landowners place their properties into conservation easements that forever restrict non-approved uses. To date, 150 private landowners have placed conservation easements on their land, permanently protecting nearly 150,000 acres. The privately held land, however, is not open for public visitation.

The ACE Basin is celebrated for being home to nine federally endangered species, including the peregrine falcon and both the leatherback and hawksbill turtles. Six federally threatened species (including the loggerhead and green turtles and the bald eagle) and 30 other statewide threatened or endangered species are located in the area, according to the DNR.

GOOD TO KNOW

NEARBY ATTRACTIONS:
The **Edisto Nature Trail** is off US Highway 17 near Highway 64 in Jacksonboro, about 15 miles west. Songbirds and Lowcountry animals frequent the area.

Caw Caw Interpretive Center (page 108)

Botany Bay Plantation Heritage Preserve (page 100)

Edisto Beach State Park (page 116)

OPTIMAL TIME TO VISIT:
In the winter to see migrating waterfowl. In spring and early summer to see other birds and wildlife.

WHAT'S UNUSUAL:
Migrating water fowl, such as wood stork, sandhill cranes, and tundra swans, as well as animals such as alligators, bald eagles, and feral hogs.

BRING:
Water and binoculars.

The ACE Basin is an incredible resource available to everyone from the hunter to the birding enthusiast. Plan a visit before the heat of the summer to see the variety of wildlife that calls this area home.

BOTANY BAY PLANTATION HERITAGE PRESERVE AND WILDLIFE MANAGEMENT AREA

1066 Botany Bay Road
Edisto Island, SC 29438
Charleston County

Immediately upon turning onto Botany Bay Road, it is clear that this tract of land is spectacular. Large live oak trees line a dusty orange dirt road, creating a thick canopy that swallows cars as their tires crunch on the uneven surface. The level of service that visitors receive is outstanding. On weekends and busy periods, guests are asked to sign in and are given a map, while an onsite volunteer offers suggestions and provides information about the property.

TO DO: **FEE: NO**

The 3,363-acre former plantation is full of history and natural beauty, and a 6.5-mile driving tour highlights everything the area has to offer. For example, the fourth stop on the tour showcases an icehouse built in the 1800s on the grounds of the former Bleak Hall Plantation. While other local Edisto families were simply attempting to eke out a living in the Edisto area, the owners of Bleak Hall Plantation traveled annually to New England on a large ship with a crew of slaves to harvest ice and transport it back to South Carolina. The ice was insulated in sawdust, and stored in the white, Victorian-style icehouse that still stands on the property. A slave cemetery also is located on the grounds of the former Bleak Hall Plantation.

Just before the icehouse, however, is a site of natural beauty that makes Botany Bay worth the visit in itself. A small parking area provides access to one of the most spectacular beaches in South Carolina. While just 12 minutes from Edisto Beach, the beaches could not look more different. Whereas Edisto is more like a typical vacation destination, with sparkling pristine beaches, perfect on which to lay a towel, the beach at Botany Bay remains natural and unmaintained. Botany Bay's beach is covered in the skeletons of dead live oak and cabbage palmetto trees. At high tide the ocean washes over the trees, while low tide leaves the trees exposed. Both times of day are truly beautiful.

Because shell collecting is outlawed at the preserve, the size and quantity of shells is truly outstanding. Visitors often will hang shells on the trees that litter the beach as a testament to the number of people who have enjoyed this beautiful location. Animals such as the endangered least tern (a small shorebird), piping plovers, and pelicans also enjoy visiting the beach. Another frequent visitor (although it only shows up in the spring and summer) is South Carolina's state reptile, the loggerhead sea turtle. This preserve hosts the second highest number of nesting loggerheads of any recorded South Carolina beach.

To get to the beach, visitors enjoy a scenic walk through the marsh via a wooden boardwalk. The walk winds through oyster beds, cordgrass, and a small, wind-battered hammock of pine trees. A maritime forest abuts the beach and has weathered the many storms that have afflicted the area. The storms, of course, have knocked down trees throughout the years, resulting in trees strewn across the beach. Some of the trees lie on their sides, leaving roots exposed and reaching into the air, and some remain rooted in the ground with

The driving tour of Botany Bay reveals remnants of the Bleak Hall Plantation that once stood here.

dry and lifeless limbs. The path to the beach is representative of all that Botany Bay has to offer, as it is both picturesque and historic. Slaves carved out the path in the 1700s with sweat and hand tools.

After or before a stroll on the beach, continue on the driving tour to explore the remaining ecosystems on the island: a large maritime forest, a picturesque marsh, a pond, a large field, and an untouched sandy beach. There is little fresh water on the island, only a small pond, and thus alligators are not as prevalent as they are in many other coastal parks. Many types of snakes live on the islands, including the eastern coral, copperhead, and cottonmouth snakes. Additionally, there are many species of

GOOD TO KNOW

NEARBY ATTRACTIONS:

Roxbury Park is a newly established park that comprises eight different ecosystems and is only 157 acres. It is home to many interesting creatures, including a pair of nesting bald eagles. The park also has great signage about local animals and plants as well as boardwalks and a house available to rent for functions or a relaxing getaway.

The **ACE Basin** is an enormous tract of land that provides hunting opportunities and trails, and is considered one of the nation's premier birding spots. For more information, see the Bear Island and Donnelly Wildlife Management areas chapter (page 96).

Edisto State Park (page 116)

OPTIMAL TIME TO VISIT:

Fall and spring, when the weather is cooler. Be aware of the tide when visiting as some prefer to stroll on the beach at low tide and others find the beauty of the submerged trees at high tide more picturesque.

WHAT'S UNUSUAL:

Visiting an undeveloped beach left largely in its natural state; the combination of history and natural beauty.

BRING:

Water and a camera.

birds. Herons and ibises frequent the marsh as they patrol for crabs in the pluff mud. Osprey soar overhead, and their nests abound on the island.

The driving tour continues past a large field before it comes to a view of the marsh, which is shaded by large live oaks draped in Spanish moss. This is where wading birds are frequently spotted. The road carries on over a dike that separates salt from brackish water. Once this dike is crossed, there is a location to put non-motorized boats into the salt marsh or Ocella Creek, the main body of freshwater that runs through the preserve. Ocella Creek feeds into the North Edisto River on its way toward the coast. Kayaking these waters provides an excellent opportunity to see crabs, little green herons, or small fish.

The map given out at Botany Bay's entrance outlines all of the historical and biological stops along the way. A beehive from 1825, the remains of an elegant plantation known for its grandeur, and remnants of the Edisto Indians that lived in this area are among the historical artifacts on the property. It is not a surprise that two separate plantations once called this barrier island home. Superior cotton was grown on the soil and the views from the plantation windows were unparalleled. The beauty of this location has not changed, making it a perfect place for nature and history lovers.

The skeleton beach is the result of Botany Bay's eroding coastline, contrasting with the island's interior where plantation buildings continue to stand, such as this ice house.

BULLS ISLAND

Ferry address:
498 Bulls Island Road
Awendaw, SC 29464
Charleston County
bullsislandferry.com

Less than an hour from the bustling streets of downtown
Charleston lies the longest stretch of undeveloped shoreline
on the East Coast: a wildlife refuge where stately snowy egrets
stalk prey among the tawny-colored spartina grass marshes and
neotropical migrating birds dart furtively through eerie maritime
forests.

TO DO: **FEE: YES**

Bulls Island receives top marks for being both the largest barrier island in the Cape Romain National Wildlife Refuge as well as a Class 1 Wilderness Area, allowing for spectacular wildlife viewing opportunities and use of pristine, desolate beaches littered by a variety of sand dollars, whelks, mollusks, and other shells. It is accessible via a short three-mile ferry ride north of Charleston, but its topography is vastly different from the developed beach resorts that populate the coastline.

Because the island remains largely undeveloped, it has no visitor accommodations except for public toilets. As such, guests should come well equipped with plenty of water, food, and insect-repellant—the mosquitos are alive and thriving at Bulls Island in the summer! The trip out to the island is generally made through Coastal Expeditions, a local company with a federal contract to ferry people to the island. The ferry has two departures on Tuesdays, Thursdays, Saturdays, and Sundays, although more information can be found on their website. The employees are very knowledgeable about marine and animal life, the island's history, and generally any local naturalist-related topic. On the way out to the island, the employees will direct visitors' attention to a variety of birds, animals, and plants along the route. Don't be surprised to stumble upon a pod of dolphins, a flock of wood storks, or a lone night heron fishing in the marsh.

The island itself is known for its dynamic edges that abruptly shift from one microenvironment to the next. Within its 5,000 acres are maritime forests, fresh and brackish water impoundments, salt marshes, and sandy beaches. Thriving in these confines are alligators, bobcats, deer, and raccoons. It is estimated that the island is home to roughly 800 American alligators, the highest alligator density outside of Florida. However, unlike in many human-populated areas in South Carolina, these gators are wary of people and provide little threat unless harassed or cornered. Tourists who encounter a group of gators lounging serenely should approach them slowly so they take the cue to vacate roads and pathways, which they will generally do. Always maintain a safe distance, especially from young gators whose watchful mother is often resting nearby, and do not harass them.

During the late 1980s, the island was used as breeding grounds for the federally endangered red wolf. This wolf was once common in the Southeast but was widely hunted until it ceased to exist in the wild. Breeding pairs on Bulls Island fostered 26 pups before the wolves

Sun-bleached trees hauntingly remain along the shore of Bulls Island, a testament to its eroding shorelines.

were relocated to North Carolina's Alligator River National Wildlife Refuge. Locals maintain some wolves swam to the mainland, hastening the breeding program's end at Bulls Island.

The island also hosts nearly 300 documented species of birds, including the federally threatened wood stork. Additionally, about half of the nation's beautiful, orange-billed oystercatchers over-winter on the island. These opportunistic birds are as adept as any local oyster shucker, patiently waiting for a bivalve to slightly open its shell before quickly inserting their blade-like bills into the mollusk and severing the muscle that allows it to close. Oystercatchers are in decline, largely due to the loss of nesting habit to sunbathers. Other noteworthy birds include black ducks, wigeons, yellow-legs, piping plovers, osprey, and eagles. Summer months can bring neotropical migrants such as the painted bunting, a bird whose brilliant hues of blue, red, and green can rival any parrot.

The ferry drops passengers off at the island's only dock, from which a path leads to the interior of the island where oaks, magnolias,

A collection of shells, skeletal remains, and other treasures make the ferry ride to Bulls Island even more interesting.

and cedars are shrouded in Spanish moss and overgrown vines. An opening reveals Dominick House, a hunting and vacation home built by New York banker Gayer Dominick in the 1920s. Prior to Dominick, 35 parties claimed ownership of Bulls Island dating back to the 1700s. At one time, Bulls Bay and the creeks behind the island are said to have been a hideout for pirates who plundered ships along the coast. During the Revolutionary War, British warships used the island as well. Dominick conveyed the land to the U.S. government in 1936 to become part of the Cape Romain National Wildlife Refuge.

Amazingly, the house survived Hurricane Hugo in 1989, a category 4 storm with devastating winds and a 20-foot tidal surge that destroyed the island's loblolly pine population and reduced the number of live oaks by a third. Prior to the storm, which completely submerged the island, the forest was considered an old-growth variety. The federal government has opted to allow the island to repopulate as it would do naturally. Most of the animal life probably perished during the storm and many new animal inhabitants are believed to have swum to the island later.

Continuing to traverse the 1.5-mile-wide island brings visitors across dikes and through forests to the jewel of Bulls Island—the magnificent Boneyard Beach. This three-mile stretch of beach is unquestionably the most photographed area of the island. Lifeless and sun-bleached oaks, cedars, and pines litter the sand in a haunting setting. The skeletonized trees are the result of a shrinking beach along the island's east side as the surf naturally erodes the sandy shoreline.

As a relatively pristine beach, this area is celebrated for its abundance of shells. Sand dollars and a variety of whelks can usually be found, and visitors are permitted to take a few home as long as live animals do not still inhabit them. The beach is shared by the federally endangered loggerhead sea turtle that lays eggs on the dunes during the early summer months, and visitors should be respectful of South Carolina's state reptile. Remnants of horseshoe, fiddler, and ghost crabs can be found during beach walks.

About 3,000 years ago, this area was home to Sewee Indians, and at least two shell middens exist on Bulls Island. Shell middens are much like current day dumps; they contain castoffs of shells and pottery shards from early Americans. These mounds are easily overlooked, as they are often just small hills adjacent to forest pathways.

On the northeast side of the island are the ruins of an old fort—modest remnants of walls built from oyster shells and sand. This fort marks where the first European settlers landed in 1670 on their

GOOD TO KNOW

NEARBY ATTRACTIONS:
Sewee Visitor and Environmental Center houses a small museum and bookstore and is home to several federally endangered red wolves.

Francis Marion National Forest has approximately 250,000 acres of land to explore, including forests and wetlands.

Explore the rest of the **Cape Romain National Wildlife Refuge** including two lighthouses, 22 miles of shoreline, and all the animals and plants that call the refuge home.

OPTIMAL TIME TO VISIT:
In the spring or fall when mosquitos are less prevalent and the weather is more accommodating.

WHAT'S UNUSUAL:
Visiting an undeveloped island left largely in its natural state; viewing Boneyard Beach; seeing a great number of alligators.

BRING:
Bug spray, a camera, and ample water.

way to Charleston. The island is named for the captain of that ship.

Bulls Island is a Class 1 Wilderness Area, one of only two on the eastern seaboard. This federal designation is given only to the most unspoiled sites, and it is carefully managed to remain primitive enough to support and attract wildlife. Come prepared to step back in time and enjoy some of South Carolina's true wilderness.

CAW CAW INTERPRETIVE CENTER

5200 Savannah Highway
Ravenel, SC 29470
Charleston County
ccprc.com/53/caw-caw-interpretive-center

Sometimes people have the tendency to overlook county parks as small, insignificant places, not worth their time, but Caw Caw Interpretive Center is a reminder of the incredible opportunities that can exist at such places. While only a county park, the amenities of this 654-acre Charleston area attraction are fantastic.

TO DO:    **FEE: YES**

Caw Caw's land was once part of an extensive system of rice plantations that dominated the South Carolina Coastal Zone, and its agricultural history is evident. The park still employs the original rice trunk system that was created to manipulate water in rice fields. However, staff now uses it to create an ideal habitat for birds. In the winter, staff flood the fields to encourage visits from wintering waterfowl. In the summer, the fields are drained to create the perfect habitat for wading birds such as egrets and herons.

Alligators thrive in the freshwater system created by these trunks. In fact, Caw Caw is considered one of the best places in the Charleston area to spot these massive reptiles lounging along the shores or swimming through freshwater canals.

Information about Caw Caw's rice plantation history can be found in the exhibit at the visitors' center. Signage, as well as hands-on components, explain the importance of rice to the area—how the fields were operated and how rice trunks function. As South Carolina was the primary American rice producer in the 1700s, places such as Caw Caw were very important to the state economy. The center also informs about the plants and animals found within the park.

Six miles of trails meander throughout the park, many of them on the elevated rice dikes created for farming. Caw Caw allowed some of the land that was used for farming to revert back to its original state—inland swamps. This allows visitors to get a feel for what the land would have looked like had it not been altered by humans. While these forests are still dense, the elevated dikes can still be spotted within their bounds. Freshwater springs and rainwater feed these swamps, which are dominated by tupelo trees and dwarf palmettos.

Oils produced by swamp plants refract sunlight, creating awe-inspiring rainbows along the boardwalk.

Caw Caw's most spectacular phenomenon can be found within this freshwater swamp system along the wooden boardwalk or the Swamp Sanctuary Trail. On sunny winter days, in the late afternoon, the sunlight can hit the swamp at just the right angle to produce a rainbow-like sheen on the water. The normally black water is transformed with a rainbow of vibrant purples, yellows, greens, and blues, which are separated into sections by thick black streaks created by the shadow of bald cypress and tupelo trees. The rainbow is so awe-inspiring, it almost looks unnatural. Oils produced by the plants dominating the swamp create a sheen on the water, which refracts sunlight hitting the water at a low angle. The only time to see this amazing array of colors is in the early winter months, primarily in January and February, on a sunny day.

While this swamp rainbow is exciting to witness, catching the display takes a bit of timing and luck. There are, however, other trails that are worth meandering along to provide expansive views of the park and glimpses of Lowcountry wildlife. Several paths skirt the former rice fields and overlook rice trunks, allowing visitors to easily choose how far they wish to walk. These trails are covered in grass and are between a half-mile and one-mile each, and they look down on the canals created by the dike system. Spanish moss hangs from the live oaks bordering these canals, and small docks and benches dot the pathways, providing great places to

watch for wildlife or take pictures. An old lifeguard chair donated from another Charleston County park sits on the grass and is a great place to view wildlife from a higher vantage point.

Many animals can be spotted within Caw Caw, including bald eagles, barred owls, osprey, otters, opossum, migrating songbirds, and waterfowl such as wood ducks. The interpretive center provides guided bird walks in the mornings, and even if a particular species does not land in the park, it may often be spotted passing overhead, for example, a pair of wood storks with their expansive black and white wings. The park has many wood duck nesting boxes that are actively used. Ducklings frequently can be seen following closely behind their mother's tail feathers in the spring months. The invasive armadillo also lives in the park near the visitors' center, and park employees can tell visitors where to look to see this new inhabitant.

One of the most picturesque trails in the park is the Maritime Forest Trail, which meanders where the forest and marsh converge. On the far side of the marsh lies a hunt club, and thus the trail provides dense forests with no views of nearby neighborhoods. A blackwater creek runs alongside this trail, separating the marsh from the forest.

A maritime forest trail, where dwarf palmetto thrives, leads visitors past marshes and a blackwater creek.

Swampy areas were chosen for rice plantations because of their abundance of water, and Caw Caw is no exception. The area was timbered in the early 1700s to create farmland and rice fields. Ownership of the land changed hands many times over the years, but it dates back to Robert Gibbes in 1703, who was South Carolina's acting governor in 1711. The last time tea was commercially grown on the site was in the early 1900s by the American Tea Growing Company.

Tea plants still thrive here, and Caw Caw hosts the only known naturalized tea colony in the United States. The name of the city of Ravenel, where the park is located, was briefly changed to Tea, South Carolina, because local residents had such high hopes for the tea industry in this region. Tea plants are easily recognizable with their plentiful large pods and their overwhelming pleasant odor. In the fall, white flowers bloom on the plants. Tea plants are labeled by the visitors' center entrance to aid in identification.

The sights and smells at Caw Caw are not to be missed. While this isn't one of the more well-known open spaces in the Charleston area, Caw Caw is a gem not only among the Charleston County Park System, but among all South Carolina's outdoor attractions.

GOOD TO KNOW

NEARBY ATTRACTIONS:

Angel Oak Park boasts a magnificent live oak tree that is over 1,500 years old and is considered the oldest living thing on the East Coast. This tree is a South Carolina treasure and one of the most spectacular sights in the state.

Dungannon Heritage Preserve is a wood stork rookery across the street from the park. In the spring, native orange lilies bloom in the park's meadows.

Botany Bay Plantation Heritage Preserve (page 100)

Edisto State Park (page 116)

OPTIMAL TIME TO VISIT:
Sunny January and February days in the late afternoon to view the rainbow effects the sun creates on the swampy water. Winter for migratory waterfowl; spring and fall for other migratory birds.

WHAT'S UNUSUAL:
Seeing the rainbow effect in the swamp, exploring a former rice plantation, seeing and smelling the dense groves of tea that are part of a naturalized, thriving tea colony.

BRING:
A camera and water.

CONGAREE NATIONAL PARK

101 National Park Road
Hopkins, SC 29061
Richland County
nps.gov/cong

Walking through the forests of Congaree National Park is akin to being transported back in time, when massive tree canopies created a primeval wonderland complete with swampy floodplains, Spanish moss, cypress knees, and a cacophony of crickets, tree frogs, owls, and woodpeckers. The park is home to an astonishing amount of biodiversity and has more than two dozen trees of state and national record-breaking sizes.

TO DO:  FEE: NO

Congaree is one of the nation's newest national park, receiving that designation in 2003. For years, it was locally referred to as Congaree Swamp, but because it does not retain water year-round, it is technically a floodplain that welcomes the overflowing waters of the Congaree River, Wateree River, and other tributaries. The periodic floods, which can occur up to 10 times a year, deposit rich silt that nourishes forest growth. Due to the difficulty of removing trees from this remote site, with its lack of navigable waters, the area was never logged. Consequently, approximately 90 tree species have reached heights and girths found nowhere else in the state, and six trees hold national records. Trees that hold national titles include laurel oak, loblolly pine, water hickory, swamp tupelo, and sweetgum. Recognized state champions include a chestnut oak, cottonwood, holly, and silver maple. Being able to view a 300-year-old loblolly pine that soars 167 feet into the sky is truly awe-inspiring. Many of the other record-holding trees, however, are harder to access, as they are often far from commonly used trails. Lightning strikes and severe storms also can alter these champion designations.

Overall, Congaree National Park is second only to the Great Smoky Mountains in the total number of tree species in any one national park. Congaree has 93 different trees on record compared to 151 in the Smokies, despite being only one-tenth of the size of its northerly neighbor. Furthermore, Congaree is top in the nation for recorded native woody vine species, boasting 26 varieties, including trumpet creeper, climbing hydrangea, peppervine, muscadine grapes, and our state flower, yellow jessamine. It has been compared to a rainforest with its diversity of tall canopy trees, vines, and understory plants.

While the bald cypresses here don't make the award-winning cuts, they still are mighty impressive. At Congaree, there are bald cypress trees with circumferences of 27.5 feet and knees as high as seven feet. Due to the incredible height of Congaree's canopy, it is considered one of the tallest temperate hardwood forests in the world and is the largest contiguous tract of old-growth bottomland hardwood forest in the country.

Pileated woodpeckers are often both seen and heard in the hardwood forest.

Lurking within this forest is also a great diversity of wildlife. Known to live at Congaree are bobcats, deer, feral pigs, coyotes, turkeys, river otters, and armadillos. It is worth noting that Congaree also is home to an abundance of mosquitos—21 different species have been identified, so it is wise

to arm yourself with some repellant. The park has a tongue-in-cheek "mosquito meter" sign near the visitors' center, warning of levels that range from mild to war zone. The still waters are perfect habitats for this pesky larvae.

Congaree encompasses 27,000 acres and is deserving of more than one visit in order to grasp all that it offers. Newcomers, however, should start with the boardwalk trail, a 2.4-mile flat hike that begins at the visitors' center and disappears deep within the forest's eerie confines. The visitors' center has trail guides that point out interesting features of the floodplain forest. The low boardwalk offers unique views of the ancient bald cypress and tupelo forest. With its dense, closed tree canopy, the forest appears ethereal. During heavy rain periods, it is not unusual for the low boardwalk to be underwater. Seldom, however, do the floodwaters block usage of the high boardwalk, which showcases a bottomland hardwood and upland pine forest. Seeing the park when it is flooded is unique, and worth a separate visit.

The Boardwalk Loop Trail leads to Weston Lake,

Common snapping turtles, such as this juvenile, have long tails and necks. They are often seen in Lake Weston.

an oxbow lake formed when the river curled back around on itself, creating a U-shaped bend. An overlook allows visitors to see the primitive long-nosed gar, a variety of turtles, including the ill-tempered snapping turtle, and an occasional snake.

Hurricane Hugo hit Congaree full force in 1989 and remnants of toppled trees are still seen throughout the upper boardwalk trail. While Congaree suffered the loss of many large trees, the hurricane naturally opened up the forest canopy, allowing seedlings to begin their lives on the forest floor.

In addition to the Boardwalk Loop Trail, the park offers about 25 miles of other marked paths that vary from 0.7 to 11 miles in length. These trails are less utilized and allow for more wildlife and bird viewing. Look for signs of feral hogs, typically in upturned, damp earth where they have rooted for plants.

Paddlers can enjoy seeing Congaree from the confines of their watercraft. For starters, there is the slow-moving Cedar Creek, a blackwater creek that barely crawls its way through the forest. Blackwater is colored by tannins in the water (rather than bacteria) and is actually very clean despite its foreboding appearance. The Congaree River marks the southern boundary of the park, and paddlers can navigate on it more than 25 miles. The best time to paddle is in late winter and early spring when rains augment water levels.

Also not to be missed are the rare and unusual synchronized firefly displays. The mass synchronization has only been documented at a few places, such as the Great Smoky Mountains National Park. Congaree's *Photinus carolinus* firefly is the same species as you see in the Smokies, but it appears in smaller numbers. These insects are visible usually late May to early June, blinking in unison and replicating holiday light displays. A call to the ranger station will verify whether the pageantry is underway. While the visitors' center is closed at night, the park remains open. Visitors should bring flashlights covered with red cellophane that create less light pollution, making the insects more visible. The fireflies can usually be seen from the boardwalk, about a quarter of a mile from the visitors' center.

Congaree rangers also lead evening "owl prowl" walks, big tree hikes, and other excursions. Many species of owls live within the park, but the most common is the barred owl. The hoot of this owl sounds as if it is asking, "Who cooks for you?" and it is the only owl that hunts during the day. It can often be seen observing the landscape silently from tree branches.

Congaree is named after a Native American tribe that once lived in the area but was decimated by smallpox in the 18th century. It has been designated a national natural landmark, a globally important bird area, and an international biosphere reserve. There are so many reasons to walk along Congaree's elevated boardwalks or among its ancient forest.

GOOD TO KNOW

NEARBY ATTRACTIONS:
Congaree Creek Heritage Preserve features short hiking trails around ponds that are home to plentiful wildlife, including alligators. Pottery shards and projectile points found there belonged to Native Americans who used the area more than 10,000 years ago.

Congaree Bluffs Heritage Preserve is a birder's paradise. Open fields are home to indigo and painted buntings, and an overlook provides great views of hawks soaring.

OPTIMAL TIME TO VISIT:
Year-round for hiking. Boaters find easier paddling after rain in late winter or early spring; the park floods after heavy rain and is truly unique but some trails may become impassable. Synchronized firefly displays are common for two weeks in late May or early June.

WHAT'S UNUSUAL:
Elevated boardwalks that allow passage through a floodplain; a wide variety of state and nationally noted large trees; and synchronized fireflies that put on a phenomenal display once a year.

BRING:
Bug spray, water, and a camera.

EDISTO BEACH STATE PARK

8377 State Cabin Road
Edisto Island, SC 29438
Colleton County
southcarolinaparks.com/edistobeach

The South Carolina coast tends to attract visitors in the blistering heat of the summer, but the real time to visit Edisto Beach State Park may be in autumn when tropical storms churn up the waters and deposit prehistoric fossils onto the shell-laden beaches. Cooler weather and fewer mosquitos allow visitors to walk the inland trails where they can visit an ancient Native American shell mound dating back to 2,000 B.C. and enjoy a maritime forest serenely draped in Spanish moss.

TO DO: 🥾 ⛺ 🎣 🏊 🔭 📷 📖 🚴 🏠 **FEE: YES**

Edisto is considered the second largest sea island on the southeastern coast with its 70 square miles at high tide—about the size of the District of Columbia. It is actually a collection of many islands connected by bridges and causeways with extensive salt marshes, a thriving maritime forest, and, of course, miles of beaches. In addition to a 1,255-acre state park, approximately 51 percent of Edisto Island is conserved through land trusts.

Fall and winter storms wreak havoc on South Carolina's coast, frequently changing the size and topography of the many barrier islands that abut the coast. These forces of nature regularly churn up areas off the coastline that were, in prehistoric times, swamps and marshes. It is here that fossils are uncovered and are subsequently washed ashore in choppy storm waves. The most spectacular discoveries have been the remains of mastodons, mammoths, and saber-tooth tigers, some of which are on display in Columbia's State Museum. Most fossils discovered tend to be shells, bone fragments, and teeth, which can be identified by their shiny, black surfaces that stand out among the pale shells on the beach. These fossils are known to date back to the late Pleistocene era.

While it's not always easy to plan trips following such storms, Edisto is worth visiting at other times as well. On virtually any day of the year, vigilant beachcombers can find sand dollars, starfish, and sharks' teeth along the shore. The latter are easily identified by their long, pointed, triangular shapes. The state park visitors' center has a variety of sharks' teeth and fossils on display for reference.

Additionally, Edisto has a large number of loggerhead sea turtles that visit in early summer to deposit their eggs in the sand dunes, resulting in a flood of hatchlings that emerge in the dead of night during the late summer. The nests are protected and clearly marked along the shore. State park rangers often schedule interpretive turtle walks where a lucky visitor can sometimes manage to catch a female laying eggs or spy new hatchlings as they race into the crashing waves.

The loggerhead is South Carolina's official state reptile. They can weigh up to 300 pounds and reach up to four feet in shell length. South Carolina averages more than 3,000 loggerhead nests yearly, and witnessing either an adult sea turtle laying eggs or the hatchlings making their way to their salty home is an amazing and rare opportunity. More common is the ability to view turtle tracks in the sand the following

Edisto has seven trails that border marshes, traverse maritime forests, and even lead visitors to an ancient Native American mound.

morning, which look like tire tracks. Disturbing a nest is a federal crime, punishable with fines and even jail time, so stay clear of any suspected nests, egg-laying females, or new hatchlings as the loggerhead is an endangered species. Turtle watch groups typically patrol Edisto in the early morning hours, marking and protecting new nesting sites. It is always exciting to see newly marked nests, which are generally designated by bright orange protective coverings and signage.

A female loggerhead sea turtle lays an average of 120 white, leathery eggs, each about the size of a pingpong ball. The temperature of the nest during incubation determines the sex of the hatchlings, which emerge at night and crawl en masse to the ocean. With a variety of predators, among them—humans, raccoons, coyotes, ghost crabs, and birds—only about one in 1,000 hatchlings will survive to sexual maturity.

Yellow sundrop flowers are favorites of the gulf fritillary butterflies that frequent coastal areas.

When the sun has taken its toll on beach-goers, it is time to explore the island forests. Gray beards of Spanish moss sway serenely from stately live oak trees throughout the forest, beckoning visitors to stroll unhurried. However, be wary of mosquitos and ticks. A good dose of bug spray is highly recommended.

Edisto Beach State Park has seven trails that range from a quarter of a mile to just over two miles, all of which are ideal for families and many of which are wheelchair accessible. The Forest Loop Trail winds through the island's maritime forest—a coastal wooded area within range of salt spray. Edisto's shaded forests feature live oaks, mature pines, palmetto palms, and bald cypress trees that expose knobby "knees" among their submerged roots. A variety of wildlife also inhabits the forests, and it is possible to discover a lazy alligator, snake, deer, or raccoon. Campers have even reported seeing a rare bobcat. (If you want to search for a bobcat, look up at the tree branches. Bobcats tend to lounge here during the day and observe diurnal action from aloft.) All of these animals prefer to avoid human contact, but visitors should stay on trails and use caution.

The Spanish Mount Trail is the longest trail, beginning at the ranger station and ending at an ancient Native American mound. It traverses through a cool canopy of live oaks and forested areas, abutting the marsh for several picturesque and scenic views. Boardwalks allow the visitor to traipse across the marshes, gathering intimate glimpses of snowy egrets, blue herons, fiddler crabs, and other wetland creatures. A quintessential odor of pluff mud invades the senses and adds to the serenity of the experience. At the end, the ancient shell midden is a bit anti-climatic, as weather and erosion have taken their toll on the hill. Edisto Indians, who historians believe were eventually wiped out by disease, constructed the mound out of oyster, mussel, and turtle shells, along with ancient pottery and bones. Essentially the mound was a dumping ground where trash and unwanted items were deposited.

The Scott Creek Trail is perhaps the park's most beautiful, beginning in the forest but quickly opening to scenic marshlands. It is short—just over a half mile—but again offers great opportunities to view wildlife and take in the iconic beauty of the island.

Kids and adults alike enjoy spending time at the park's interpretive center, a building that features stuffed animals, displays of live reptiles, fossils, and many hands-on exhibits such as live whelk and horseshoe and hermit crabs.

Edisto Beach State Park offers great opportunities to enjoy a variety of ecosystems and partake in an assortment of activities. Visit the park off-season to be pleasantly surprised at what it offers.

GOOD TO KNOW

NEARBY ATTRACTIONS:
Edisto Island Serpentarium, located at 1374 Highway 174, has reptiles in outdoor gardens and an indoor solarium, including snakes, lizards, turtles, and alligators.

Botany Bay Plantation Heritage Preserve (page 100)

Caw Caw Interpretive Center (page 108)

The **ACE Basin** is an enormous tract of land that provides hunting opportunities and trails, and is considered one of the nation's premier birding spots. For more information, see the Bear Island and Donnelly Wildlife Management areas chapter (page 96).

OPTIMAL TIME TO VISIT:
In the fall to find prehistoric fossils along the beach, avoid summer crowds, and take in all the island has to offer.

WHAT'S UNUSUAL:
The opportunity to find prehistoric fossils; wheelchair accessible paths; a native American shell mound.

BRING:
A bathing suit, hiking shoes, and water.

FRANCIS BEIDLER FOREST

336 Sanctuary Road
Harleyville, SC 29448
Dorchester County

Situated in the 45,000-acre Four Holes Swamp, Francis Beidler Forest is home to a plethora of plants and animals. The forest and wildlife sanctuary, which is owned by the Audubon Society, occupies around 16,000 of those acres and offers an elevated boardwalk of 1.75 miles that allows visitors to meander through its old-growth forest.

TO DO: 🚶 🛶 👓 📷   **FEE: YES**

The forest consists mainly of tupelo gum and bald cypress trees with a sprinkling of other varieties, such as pines and maples, in the areas that are less water-logged. The boardwalk is accessed through the visitors' center, and informative self-guided pamphlets should be collected here. The guide points out important landmarks, with corresponding numbers along the trail, such as the largest cypress knee that is visible from the boardwalk. Knees are looping roots that project above the earth's surface, some as high as several feet above the ground. Their purpose is unknown, although the predominant theory argues that they anchor the tree in the soil.

The two principal trees in the park, cypress and tupelo gum trees, can be difficult to tell apart as they look similar in structure, contain knees, and are deciduous. Tupelo tree trunks typically grow very straight with branches coming out at right angles. Additionally, tupelo trees tend to fan out at the base whereas cypress trees widen in a rounded fashion at their foundation. The name "bald cypress" refers to the fact that this tree loses its leaves in the winter and thus becomes "bald." Conifers such as cypress trees tend to be evergreen; however, as the bald cypress tree illustrates, deciduous conifers do exist.

The Four Holes Swamp in Francis Beidler Forest is comprised of blackwater that is rich in nutrients and is actually clean, in spite of its foreboding tint. The color is derived from tannins in the water, rather than bacteria. The swamp mimics a river, and its water runs for more than 60 miles before it joins the Edisto River near the coast. The water in Francis Beidler Forest helps make up Charleston's ACE Basin, a large water basin that feeds the majority of the coast.

Visitors should venture along the boardwalk slowly as animals are plentiful but easy to miss in the dark brown palette of the forest. A dry erase board in the visitors' center identifies animals that have been seen or heard on the trail that day and is a good starting point for finding wildlife. The employees in the visitors' center are also very knowledgeable about the animal activity in the forest.

Some of the most notable residents of Francis Beidler Forest include the alligator and the barred owl. While it is

Barred owls can be found silently perched in trees, hunting for crawfish in the swamp below.

GOOD TO KNOW

NEARBY ATTRACTIONS:
Givhans Ferry State Park allows visitors to explore the Edisto River, the longest blackwater river in the United States.

OPTIMAL TIME TO VISIT:
Fall or spring mornings to see the many birds that use the forest as part of their migration path; the earlier in the day, the better.

WHAT'S UNUSUAL:
Francis Beidler Forest has the largest stand of virgin tupelo gum and cypress trees in the world and incredible diversity of fauna.

BRING:
Bug spray, water, and a bird guide.

see the barred owl on the boardwalk (the location of his nest is identified on the visitors' center guide), you will probably hear his unique call, which sounds as if he is hooting, "who, who, who cooks for you." The barred owl is the only owl that hunts during daylight and, therefore, visitors often hear or spy this majestic bird.

Bobcats, whitetail deer, foxes, river otters, beavers, and several different types of bats are among the many mammals that inhabit the park. However, as the Audubon Society owns the wildlife sanctuary, it is no surprise that the birds are the main draw. Keep a sharp eye out for ibises poking their beaks into the mud or anhinga sunning their wings on broken logs. Egrets, several types of herons, common loons, woodpeckers, and wood storks frequent the park as well. Migrants, such as warblers, are common to the park, especially on warm spring mornings. The best place to spot hawks is in the trees above Sanctuary Road—the dirt road that leads to the visitors' center. It is common to see at least two hawks here on any given day. Red-tailed hawks, red-shouldered hawks, Cooper's hawks, and sharp-shinned hawks all reside in the park.

rare to spot an alligator in the swamp's blackwater river, one can frequently be seen hanging out in or near Goodson Lake, which is located about halfway along the boardwalk trail. An elevated lookout tower is perched at the edge of the lake to allow visitors to survey the area for turtles or inspect the trees for birds, such as wood storks, that can sometimes be found perching on tree limbs. Spanish moss also dangles at eye level from this vantage point. If you don't

Other wildlife include tree frogs, turtles, dragon- and damselflies, gar, eels, and crayfish. There are 36 varieties of crayfish in our state, but if you can't see them among the rocks and leaves in the swamp, look for the lumpy mud towers along the shores. When not scavenging in the water for food, some crayfish burrow into the mud, creating distinctive mud chimneys that give away their locations. The Audubon website has an extremely detailed list of the flora and fauna found in the park, and it is definitely worthwhile to peruse the website before visiting.

About 1,800 of the 16,000 acres in Francis Beidler Forest are part of an old-growth forest. Some of the cypress trees in the park are more than 1,000 years old, resulting in immense knees and sizeable trunks. Enormous cypress knees spring up all around the boardwalk, some more than a foot in diameter and over seven feet tall. The cypress trees and knees here are larger than the ones easily visible in Congaree National Park. Francis Beidler Forest has the largest stand of virgin tupelo gum and cypress trees in the world, which resulted in its

categorization as a National Natural Landmark in 1979.

The Audubon Society offers early morning guided walks, emphasizing bird species, as well as guided canoe trips through the forest. Both of these provide a much more in-depth look at the park than walking it alone would, especially the canoe trips, which allow visitors a chance to explore otherwise inaccessible parts of the swamp.

The Boardwalk Trail leads visitors into Four Holes Swamp where old-growth bald cypress and tupelo gum trees abound.

HUNTING ISLAND STATE PARK

2555 Sea Island Parkway
Hunting Island, SC 29920
Beaufort County
southcarolinaparks.com/huntingisland

There is a reason why Hunting Island is the most visited state park in South Carolina: from its sandy beaches to its dense maritime forest, it exemplifies the best of what the famous South Carolina coast has to offer. Hunting Island is a 5,000-acre barrier island located in the Lowcountry near the beautiful and historic town of Beaufort.

TO DO: 🥾 ⛺ 🏊 🎣 🔭 📷 📖 🚴 🏠   **FEE: YES**

Originally built in the 1930s, Hunting Island is one of 16 South Carolina parks developed by the Civilian Conservation Corps (CCC). The landscape of the park remains natural as rangers have opted to leave the beach completely untouched, allowing fallen trees and washed up logs to remain where they land until they decompose or are carried out to sea.

Visitors should keep an eye out for wildlife from the moment that they enter the park. A drive through the maritime forest leads to the visitors' center that has information about all the island has to offer, including trail maps. Several small ponds lie between the parking lot and the visitors' center where it is common to see the scaly nose or the beady eyes of an American alligator staring up through dense patches of duckweed.

One of the most spectacular features of Hunting Island State Park is the maritime forest. While most South Carolina maritime forests have smaller, wind-battered palmettos, Hunting Island is unique in the size of the trees that abut the beach. Full-size palmettos greet the sand in thick groves, a result of the intense erosion that takes place here. It is amazing to see the forest suddenly cut off, exposing the fine, white sand beaches. Boardwalks meander through the trees and guide visitors to the beach through this forest. If guests are looking for a longer path, the park offers additional trails for biking or hiking through the forest.

The state park offers an extensive trail system, totaling more than eight miles in length. The trails are all interconnected, allowing visitors to choose a path as long or short as they desire. Trails meander through the forest or marsh, or lead up the beach, showing the diverse topography of Hunting Island. One of the most picturesque hikes is the Marsh Boardwalk Trail, which provides the chance to walk across the marsh on a wooden boardwalk and then negotiate a small island. This is considered one of the best places to view a sunset from within the park. It is a great place to enjoy the salt marsh without getting wet feet. In this area, marsh birds are plentiful, including great white egrets, great blue herons, and wood storks, as well as clapper rails and marsh wrens.

The only publicly accessible lighthouse in the state of South Carolina rests on Hunting Island's grassy knoll. A black and white color-blocked lighthouse rises above the trees on the island and is an iconic symbol of the park. A small

It's well worth climbing the 175 steps of the state's only publicly-accessible lighthouse to witness a beautiful island view.

green field and white picket fence surround the beacon, creating an iconic, picturesque view. It is well worth the extra fee to climb the 175 iron steps to the top of the lighthouse for the outstanding views. Because of imminent beach erosion on barrier islands such as Hunting Island, the lighthouse was built to be easily dismantled and reassembled by taking apart the transposable cast-iron sections. Since its construction, it

GOOD TO KNOW

NEARBY ATTRACTIONS:
Beaufort is a coastal town rich in history, wonderful food, plentiful art galleries and antique shops, and a bayside park.

OPTIMAL TIME TO VISIT:
In the fall to explore the maritime forest without a swarm of mosquitos.

WHAT'S UNUSUAL:
The large, dense maritime forest; the climbable lighthouse; a large saltwater lagoon.

BRING:
Bug spray and water.

has already been moved once—1.3 miles inward in 1889.

Of course, the pristine beaches on Hunting Island also are marvelous. The sand is superfine and ivory in color, and the water is among the clearest in South Carolina. Five miles of beaches stretch around the island, perfect for sunbathing or strolling. Birds such as piping plovers run along the shore, and pelicans soar above. For those who want to venture further out into the ocean, the park also has a boat ramp.

For a quieter waterfront spot, the saltwater lagoon, created in 1968 by sand dredging, is the place to be. Fishing, kayaking, or floating on the placid water is common here, and it is a great place to spot wading birds or small mammals. The lagoon is accessed by a 1.4-mile trail. Hunting Island park rangers have even observed unusual species such as seahorses and barracuda here.

Another gem in the park is the interpretive center located near a long fishing pier that overlooks Fripp Inlet. Rangers here show guests live animals, skulls, bones, and other animal remains; and taxidermy animals are displayed for educational purposes. Stroll out along the fishing pier where locals

Once listed as an endangered species, the American alligator now thrives in the plentiful ponds at Hunting Island.

and visitors alike often go crabbing or fishing. The interpretive center will even loan rods and reels to visitors. Ospreys and pelicans frequently soar overhead as well. The fishing pier additionally overlooks a marsh where animals commonly search for food. Lucky guests may see a raccoon strolling through the cordgrass or a great white egret standing out against the bright green background.

For those who want more than a day trip at Hunting Island, there are lodging opportunities available on the island.

While the majority of the cabins have been lost to erosion, the state park still has one that is available for rent, offering great views of the lighthouse. Most visitors, however, choose to sleep in the great outdoors at one of the 181 campsites adjacent to the Atlantic Ocean. Many of the sites are shaded oceanfront locations that have electrical hookups and access to restrooms with hot water. As Hunting Island has so many amazing trails and beautiful miles of beaches to explore, staying at least one night is a marvelous idea.

HUNTINGTON BEACH STATE PARK

16148 Ocean Highway
Murrells Inlet, SC 29576
Georgetown County
southcarolinaparks.com/huntingtonbeach

Nestled directly below bustling Myrtle Beach is Huntington Beach State Park, a quiet oasis that is home to sandy shores, a variety of animals, and a 30-room castle open for tours. This 2,500-acre park has several different walking trails, fresh and salt water, and miles of pristine beaches to explore.

TO DO: 🚶 ⛺ 🏊 🎣 🔭 📷 📖   **FEE: YES**

The splendor of the park is evident immediately from the entrance that takes visitors across an expansive causeway separating saltwater from a brackish pond. This drive is a great place to see alligators and wading birds. Cars are prohibited from stopping on the causeway, but there is a parking lot on the far side to permit visitors to return to the elevated road. Pedestrian paths line both sides of the causeway, and small piers that are ideal for viewing and photography overlook both water areas. Alligators frequently lounge in the brackish pond and sun themselves on the small islands that are exposed during low tide.

The walk across the causeway is part of what rangers refer to as "the square," a two-mile loop trail that explores several of the ecosystems within the park. The trail not only provides access to South Beach, a picturesque South Carolina beach perfect for sunbathing, but it also borders two brackish ponds, both of which are packed full of alligators. Huntington Beach State Park has one of the largest alligator populations in the State Park Systems, and gators can be seen crossing the path or lounging between the cordgrass in the pond. During Myrtle Beach Bike Week in May, the gators are especially active, as the rumbling of motorcycles is remarkably

similar to the mating growl of alligators. Should cyclists drive across the causeway, the gators often become very excitable, and males will rear up in the water or thrash around vigorously.

Tours of Atalaya castle are available for a fee.

Just to the left of the causeway is the park's nature center, which is a must see. The center has knowledgeable volunteers on staff who can answer many questions about the park, and it features several different live exhibits. A touch tank houses stingrays, sea stars, and hermit crabs. Additionally, a baby alligator lives in the freshwater tank in the nature center, and although visitors cannot touch it, there is an opportunity to get up-close and personal with these notoriously private reptiles. One of the big draws of the nature center, however, is the view of the bald eagles nesting within the park's boundary. The eagles nest directly across from the nature center in a tall pine tree, and the staff placed a powerful birding scope at the window to provide a perfect view into the nest. Bald eagles add to their nests every year, so the nests are

GOOD TO KNOW

NEARBY ATTRACTIONS:

Brookgreen Gardens is located across the street from Huntington Beach State Park and contains many of the sculptures that Anna Hyatt Huntington created while living in the Atalaya Castle. The garden exudes Southern charm with its spidery live oak trees and plentiful flowers.

Myrtle Beach State Park is about 15 miles from Huntington Beach, and while it's a small park that's main draw is a strip of beach close to Myrtle's Grand Strand, it is home to many interesting animals such as sea turtles and owls. Check the state park website or Facebook for information about animals currently residing in the park. (Screech owls commonly nest near the visitors' center.)

Waccamaw National Wildlife Refuge contains approximately 55,000 acres of trails through wetlands and longleaf pine forests.

OPTIMAL TIME TO VISIT:
In the fall to see spoonbills or during Bike Week in May to experience gator growls.

WHAT'S UNUSUAL:
Large concentrations of alligators; roseate spoonbills in the summer and fall; bald eagles; a mixture of attractions: a jetty, a castle, marshes, and pristine beaches.

BRING:
Water and a bathing suit.

very large and elaborate. The eagles generally lay eggs in the dead of winter, and so it is usually necessary to visit in early spring to catch the eaglets in the nest.

A short trail, which is really just a long boardwalk, leaves from the nature center. The Kerrigan Nature Trail is a 0.3-mile out-and-back path that extends into a lagoon via a boardwalk. Visitors can spot the bald eagle nest from the end of the boardwalk with strong binoculars, but other birds are prolific in this area as well. Green herons, snowy egrets, and great blue herons fish on the exposed oyster beds in the marsh, looking for small fish and crabs. From late July through October, visitors may be lucky enough to spot roseate spoonbills fishing in the marsh. These pink birds with rounded bills are rare in South Carolina and a beautiful addition to the park.

Another great walk in the park is the Sandpiper Pond Trail, a two-mile out-and-back trail with sandy soil that ambles alongside a saltwater pond teeming with loons and grebes. The trail passes many different overlooks that peer into the lagoon, across the nearby dunes, and onto the sandy beach. The path also snakes through a grove of wind-battered live oaks as well as cedars and pines draped with Spanish moss.

One end of the trail begins across from the nature center and another end of the trail provides access to North Beach. A three-mile walk from the North Beach parking lot also takes visitors to the Murrell's Inlet jetty, which is a great place to spot shorebirds. Birds land on the jetty and fly in swarms around it as fishermen try to catch dinner. Sapphire water crashes against the rocks of the jetty, a paved strip of land that extends into the Atlantic, creating a scenic and breezy walking environment.

The park's final landmark is the nationally historic castle, Atalaya, which holds many treasures within its walls. Renowned sculptor Anna Hyatt Huntington and her husband, author Archer Huntington, built this Moorish-style castle in 1931, using it as their home. Inspired by Spanish architecture, the Huntingtons constructed this beachfront oasis in order to escape frigid Northern winters. The castle features both indoor and outdoor sculpting rooms as well as an oyster shucking room, stables, two large courtyards, and servant quarters. For a small fee, visitors can explore the building and grounds of this lavish former home. In building and maintaining their elaborate structure, the Huntingtons created many local jobs, vitally improving the local economy. Anna Huntington also fashioned many sculptures here, a variety of which can now be seen across the street at Brookgreen Gardens. The state park actually sits on property owned by Brookgreen Gardens and leased to the state since 1960.

Huntington Beach State Park is truly unique in the amount of diverse activities it has to offer. It is easy to spend an entire day in the park. From hiking to birdwatching to sunbathing, there is so much to do in this large and beautiful park.

Great blue herons enjoy fishing in the park's many ponds and wetlands.

LEWIS OCEAN BAY HERITAGE PRESERVE

S.C. 90 and International Road
Conway, SC 29526
Horry County

Although just 30 minutes from the high-rise hotels and amusement park rides of Myrtle Beach, Lewis Ocean Bay is a world apart from one of South Carolina's most famous tourist destinations. The preserve is difficult to find, as only a "Wildlife Viewing Area" sign denotes its existence off Highway 90, but the turn-off is worth taking for a chance to view some of the state's rare plants and unusual habitats. And, fortunately, a kiosk at the preserve's parking lot will further explain all that this preserve has to offer.

TO DO: **FEE:** NO

The majority of Lewis Ocean Bay is a longleaf pine savanna habitat, providing an environment for grassland plants such as the flowering colicroot, a plant with beautiful white blossoms, and savanna camas with its bright purple blossoms. Longleaf pines are a fire-dependent species and thus the preserve sometimes conducts controlled burnings. The burnings clear the land of brush to allow grassland species to thrive and seed pods to open for germination. Other plants that grow in this region are either fire-resistant or fire-dependent. Wildflowers, such as wild indigo, orange milkwort, and the rare spreading pogonia orchid, grow profusely during the spring and summer months. Cinnamon ferns and bracken ferns are prevalent beneath longleaf and pond pines, creating a prehistoric-looking expanse of land. A slow-moving blackwater creek also wanders along the roadways.

The big draw of the heritage preserve, however, are the multitude of carnivorous plants that grow here. These plants thrive in nutrient-poor soil by drawing excess nutrients from insects that they consume. The dwarf sundew, a small, fire-engine red plant with bulbous leaves that sport mucus-covered tentacles, grows close to the ground and entices insects with its bright coloring and sweet nectar. Tiny insects get stuck on the glandular hairs, which curl around the bugs and suffocate them before digesting them.

Three species of pitcher plants—frog's britches, hooded pitcher plants, and trumpet pitcher plants—also grow in clumps at the preserve. Visitors should look for them sticking out amongst the grass along the roadside. Each of these pitcher plants has huge flowers that bloom from April to June. The hooded and trumpet pitcher plants have yellow flowers with droopy petals, whereas frog britches have rusty red blooms that seem to resemble a pair of short pants hanging out to dry. The flowers are slightly smaller than a human fist and are just as dramatic as the pitcher plants themselves with their tall columnar structures. Pitcher plants have long tubes lined in nectar that trap insects and even small frogs. The tubes narrow as they get closer to the ground and are often filled with rainwater, which allows insects to either become trapped or drown within the structure.

The most famous plant within the confines of the preserve, however, is the Venus flytrap, a very specialized plant that grows naturally only in the Coastal Plain of North and South Carolina. While the plant is more prevalent in North Carolina near Wilmington, a small population does thrive in Lewis Ocean Bay

The hood of the pitcher plant keeps water from filling its trumpet where insects are ingested.

Heritage Preserve. Most people have only seen this carnivorous plant in nurseries, with its prickly leaves that snap closed when an insect lands inside; they are difficult to find in the wild. Sadly, the plant is unmarked and tough to locate without a knowledgeable guide, as the preserve has had issues with theft in the past. Yet, to catch a glimpse of the plants with tall white flowers and green clapping leaves with red interiors is truly fantastic. These Venus flytraps, along with pitcher plants and spreading pogonia orchids, are generally located at the cross section of Target and Old Kingston roads. Visitors should park on the edge of the road to explore. While there are two designated parking areas within the park, visitors may temporarily pull off on the side of the road as the preserve generally is not crowded.

The name of the preserve stems from the prevalence of Carolina bays within its borders. Carolina bays are egg-shaped depressions found on the coastal plains of South and North Carolina. Originally South Carolina possessed nearly 4,000 Carolina bays, but currently only 400 remain intact, ranging in size from one to more than 1,000 acres. The origin of these bays, which are all angled from the

GOOD TO KNOW

NEARBY ATTRACTIONS:

Waccamaw National Wildlife Refuge is a 23,000-acre preserve in Horry County that abounds with outdoor activities from paddling to hiking. More information can be found on the U.S. Fish and Wildlife Service's website.

Huntington Beach State Park (page 128) and **Myrtle Beach State Park** (page 130) are only 30 minutes away.

OPTIMAL TIME TO VISIT:

In the spring to see wildflowers blooming.

WHAT'S UNUSUAL:

Many different types of carnivorous plants, a large colony of black bears, and beautiful wildflowers.

BRING:

Water and a camera.

southeast to the northwest and often are filled with water, are unknown. Heavy research, including radiation dating, has led to the most commonly accepted theory that the bays were shaped by wind activity. Lewis Ocean Bay Heritage Preserve has the largest collection of Carolina bays of any heritage preserve, boasting 23 bays within its nearly 10,000 acres. The foliage around these bays is dense with plants, such as the sweet smelling red bay, and thus it is hard to get up close to their shores.

Frequent visitors to these bays are coastal black bears, which thrive within Lewis Ocean Bay. The preserve has the highest concentration of coastal black bears within the state, and even if they are not always visible, visitors often can hear the low growl of a bear as it meanders among the several species of blueberries and huckleberries that grow close to Carolina bays. Especially on hot days, bears like to curl up next to the cooler shores of Carolina bays and snack on the edible plants that grow thickly in these areas. The Department of Natural Resources estimates that around 32 bears live on the preserve, and its staff is in the midst of a four-year research project that involves trapping, collaring, and monitoring the bears in the preserve.

Another species that brings visitors to the park is the red-cockaded woodpecker, a federally threatened species that is largely disappearing due to the decline in its habitat: longleaf pine forests. The birds are very elusive, but white bands on the bottom of longleaf pine trees mark active nests. (For more information about these birds, see the chapter on the Carolina Sandhills National Wildlife Refuge, pg 78.)

The longleaf pine savanna at Lewis Bay has a diversity of plants that thrive when maintained through controlled burns.

There are no real trails within the preserve, but visitors are encouraged to sightsee from the roads within the park, either on foot or from a vehicle. Horses also are permitted in the preserve; however, some roads are open to foot traffic only—no horses or vehicles. When wandering, visitors might come across artillery shells littering the ground, as the preserve was once a bombing range.

Lewis Bay Ocean Heritage Preserve is truly an unexplored gem on South Carolina's northern shore. Rare plants, large mammals, and a variety of butterflies, from gulf fritillaries and sulphur butterflies to migrating monarchs, await visitors at this unusual coastal preserve.

LIGHTHOUSE INLET HERITAGE PRESERVE

A little past 1711 East Ashley Avenue
East Folly Beach, SC
Charleston County

The ocean meets the marsh at East Folly Beach, forming a peaceful inlet that abounds with iconic South Carolina images. It is an ideal place to take a beach walk, absorb coastal scenes, and spot the dolphins and birds that call this area home.

TO DO: 🥾 🛶 🎣 🔭 📷 📖 🚴   **FEE: NO**

Limited street parking is available near the preserve so it may be difficult to visit during the summer months when tourists flock to Folly Beach. The preserve is most enjoyable in the fall or spring when coastal South Carolina is cooler and more inviting to outdoor exploration.

The preserve derives its name from the abandoned lighthouse that sits offshore on the now submerged Morris Island. This barrier island once bordered Folly Island, but erosion caused Morris Island to disappear. A large sandbar surfaces at low tide, the last remnant of the island that was once so established that it contained not only the Morris Island Light, but many houses as well. The lighthouse was built in 1767 and decommissioned in 1962. Local fundraising efforts have maintained the lighthouse, which was once in danger of being demolished. Made of brick arranged in red and white stripes, the tower stands 161 feet tall, and a reinforced steel structure around the base protects it from the waves that constantly crash around it. The metal beacon, two large windows, and the entrance are visible from the heritage preserve. It is not accessible because it sits offshore, but the heritage preserve is considered the best place to marvel at its beauty. This site is so picturesque that it often draws photographers and young couples for engagement photo sessions.

A sandbar visible at low tide is the only remnant of the now-submerged Morris Island on which a lighthouse still stands tall.

Farther up the coast, another tall, thin structure is visible. This is the Sullivan's Island Light, more commonly known as the Charleston Light, built when the Morris Island Light was decommissioned. This lighthouse is much more modern and even contains an elevator, which climbs the black and white wooden structure.

Because the preserve sits on an inlet where salt and brackish water meet, plant and animal life are quite diverse. From the parking lot, visitors will walk a paved path that traverses a small maritime forest with stunted, wind-battered pine and palmetto trees. The shrubbery in this region is dense and thus supports great bird life. Baltimore orioles, boat-tailed grackles, and even painted buntings may chirp and flit amongst these trees, and birders may find themselves stopping frequently to whip out binoculars.

The paved path leads to a sandy one that climbs dunes to reach the seashore. Signage offers information on the area, including the birds and shells that can be found within the preserve. Arrival at

GOOD TO KNOW

NEARBY ATTRACTIONS:
Folly Beach County Park is located on the other side of Folly Island and is another example of the converging marsh and ocean ecosystems. A fee is required to park here.

Angel Oak Park, only a half hour away, boasts a magnificent live oak tree that is more than 1,500 years old and is considered the oldest living thing on the East Coast. This tree is a South Carolina treasure and a must-see.

Caw Caw Interpretive Center (page 108)

OPTIMAL TIME TO VISIT:
Spring and fall for migratory birds.

WHAT'S UNUSUAL:
Seeing a historic, offshore lighthouse, an untouched South Carolina beach, the plethora of plants and animals within two merging ecosystems, and a bird sanctuary.

BRING:
A camera and water.

the beach instantly provides views of the Morris Island Lighthouse, as well as of dead, bleached oak trees that litter the sand. The high tide line is marked by yellow marsh grass that is washed up with the waves. The beach is unmanaged and thus no downed trees are removed, creating a natural South Carolina shore that only adds to the beauty of the preserve.

At high tide it can be difficult to walk along the preserve. The waves crash close to the forest that abuts the beach. At low tide, however, visitors can walk down the beach and observe the ocean on one side and the marsh on the other. The marsh is roped off, as it is a protected bird area. Shorebirds nest along the spartina grass that covers the ground, and it is not uncommon to see egrets perched in the few pine trees that dot the marsh, or view one wading in the water, poised to grab a small fish.

The heritage preserve is a favorite spot for fishermen as fish are prevalent in inlets where different types of water merge. For this reason, pods of dolphins commonly swim offshore, their fins surfacing every several minutes. Pelicans also love this area and congregate in large flocks offshore. They can be seen soaring overhead then catapulting their bodies into the water when they spot a fish.

At low tide, the water recedes, revealing enormous oyster beds near the shore. It is truly unique to be able to walk along the edge of a barrier island such as Folly. Two beautiful ecosystems—the marsh and the beach—converge and create a spectacular sight.

Swimming is forbidden in this preserve due to dangerous currents. Fishing (with a license), tanning, walking, bird watching, and shell collecting are all permitted on this land that is owned by the Charleston County Park System and managed by the Department of Natural Resources.

The beginning of the path passes the foundations of former seaside homes that were lost to the war against eroding shorelines, a common problem for barrier islands. Groins and jetties, built to help prevent the erosion that continues to claim still more property, also are visible but do not distract from the beauty of the natural elements.

The Lighthouse Heritage Preserve contains sea oats, palmetto trees, and dwarf palms, among other plants that are emblematic of the Carolina shore. Visitors may walk the three miles of shoreline, and if they are looking for an even longer hike, the beach continues to the west, past the large, brightly colored houses that tourists love to rent during the summer.

The beach on the east end of Folly Beach has much to offer outdoor enthusiasts. Animal life, picturesque natural beaches, and an abandoned lighthouse are among the highlights that draw thousands of people to this beach every year.

Sun-bleached trees are evidence of an eroding coastline where plant life is stymied by encroaching saltwater.

PEACHTREE ROCK HERITAGE PRESERVE

883 Peachtree Rock Road
Lexington, SC 29073
Lexington County

Peachtree Rock may have fallen off its pedestal when its fragile base collapsed in 2013, leaving the giant limestone rock on its side, but the dynamic ecosystem of this heritage preserve still warrants a visit to examine fossilized seashells, endangered plants, and unusual sandstone formations.

TO DO:    **FEE: NO**

The Sandhills region of the state is a souvenir of the Eocene Epoch, roughly 50 million years ago when ocean levels were about 500 feet higher and beaches dominated what is now the fall line of the state. When the water receded, sandstone was created. Exposed bits of sandstone have, for the most part, been dissolved by wind and rain. Peachtree Rock is unusual in that some of these sandstone outcroppings were sheltered by ironstone, a harder sedimentary rock that acted like an umbrella to protect the sandstone directly beneath it. The exposed sandstone unmasks fossilized bivalves, shrimp shells, and shrimp burrows. While these remnants are small in size, this is considered South Carolina's largest marine fossil location as well as the state's largest sandstone outcropping. It is also proof that the Sandhills region of the state once harbored marine life and a more tropical climate.

The iconic namesake is only about a half-mile from the parking lot. It was once a massive, stand-alone formation whose lower layers eroded to create an upside-down pyramid that defied gravity. The perilously balanced rock, which resembled a 20-foot-tall peach in appearance, suddenly toppled in 2013. Most believe natural forces finally eroded the fragile sandstone base and caused its spill but, undoubtedly, human hands that have carved and scraped at the rock for years had a role in its demise. (Vandalism and graffiti are a problem at this preserve.) Many hope the rock will one day be housed in a special exhibit that will protect it from being completely eaten away by the elements.

Deeper into the preserve is Little Peachtree Rock, a smaller twin that overlooks a hilly area of the park. While less impressive in size, it is still interesting to see the sandstone exposed under its protective rock layer.

Mountain laurel, a plant normally seen in higher elevations, is found here.

While the preserve is named for the iconic sandstone formation, this natural wonder is merely the tip of all that Peachtree Rock Heritage Preserve offers. This 460-acre preserve boasts the Midlands' only existing, albeit small, waterfall. It is also home to a variety of endangered and threatened plants, and it has several unusual micro-environments. There are about 15 miles of trails that frequently crisscross each other, so it is easy to see nearly all the preserve has to offer without too much walking.

Traipsing past Peachtree Rock brings hikers to a bowl-shaped area at the base of a small sandstone cliff. This is where the diminutive Hunt Creek

The iconic Peachtree Rock has fallen off its spindle base, although Little Peachtree Rock is still balancing perilously at this heritage preserve.

plummets 20 feet, an anomaly in the flat landscape made possible by a dense rocky area that retains water above the normal water table. The trickle of water splashes down the cliff to an assortment of moisture-loving plants, including the cranefly orchid. This orchid bears leaves in the winter and spring that die back in the summer. Then, sans foliage, the orchid suddenly sprouts a four- to 20-inch spike of small, pale purple flowers in late summer and early fall. Also found in this area are several species of ferns and northern red salamanders. If nothing else, this waterfall offers a cool respite to Columbia's staggering summer heat.

This zone is framed by a swamp tupelo and evergreen bog with mountain laurels, swamp titi, and skunkweed. Skunkweed, named for the subtle odor it emits when it blooms, is normally found in cool mountain areas and not in the center of the state's low-lying plateau. Carnivorous pitcher plants and sundew also grow in nearby seepage bogs.

Leaving the waterfall, the trail runs along small sandstone cliffs and ascends to the preserve's high point. This is a sandy, dry area completely divergent from the boggy river bottom, although it is only about one mile away. Here turkey oaks, sparkleberry bushes, and longleaf pines grow in abundance. The preserve, like most of the Southeast, lost its original old-growth longleaf pine forest to the timber and turpentine industries in the 19th century. The non-native slash pine species was removed in 2007, and the area was replanted with longleaf pine seedlings, which are particularly slow growing. This area continues to thrive and resemble its natural state thanks to prescribed burns and volunteer help. Also among these trees is the federally endangered Rayner's blueberry bush, although only a keen eye will be able to discern it among the other shrubs. The preserve is only one of three areas known to produce this rare fruit. Another rare species in the preserve is the Sandhills rosemary, a beautiful, aromatic bush.

Farther along the trail, the observant hiker can detect the ruins of an old moonshine still. This rusting, barrel-shaped apparatus is thought to date back to the 1930s. During Prohibition, the demand for moonshine increased dramatically, and corn-based alcohols were often produced in rural areas near water sources. Later, stills continued to be utilized to manufacture whiskey, allowing producers to avoid high alcohol taxes. Revenue officers who discovered a moonshine operation would frequently use an axe to puncture and destroy the still, rendering it useless. Look closely at this antique and you'll see signs of destruction that make one suspect this scenario might have played out here. Native Americans once used this site as well, and shards of pottery have been found within the confines of the park.

With its variety of landscapes, Peachtree Rock Heritage Preserve is also home to many different types of birds, from common songbirds to black vultures, red-cockaded woodpeckers, pine warblers, and the more elusive yellow-billed cuckoos.

The Nature Conservancy purchased the original 375 acres of this preserve in the 1970s for its geological and biological diversity. Adjacent land was later added to the site by the state. The State Department of Natural Resources and the local arm of the Nature Conservancy currently manage the preserve jointly.

In 1976 South Carolina became the first state to create a heritage trust program to protect critically endangered habitats. These preserves remain largely undeveloped and are often underutilized, but each has been selected for the plants, animals, and geology that make South Carolina unusual. As of 2008, more than 83,000 acres have been set aside in the state. The preserves are open to the public during daylight hours. As is typical of preserves, Peachtree Rock has no public facilities.

GOOD TO KNOW

NEARBY ATTRACTIONS:
Shealy's Pond Heritage Preserve, less than 15 minutes away, is known for its old-growth Atlantic white cedar stand, an unusual Atlantic Coast variety that has largely been depleted in South Carolina. This site also contains a variety of carnivorous plants, several miles of trails, and a small, beautiful mill pond.

OPTIMAL TIME TO VISIT:
Year-round.

WHAT'S UNUSUAL:
Sandstone formations that house shell and shrimp remnants and the Sandhills region's only waterfall.

BRING:
Water, camera.

PINCKNEY ISLAND NATIONAL WILDLIFE REFUGE

Pinckney Wildlife Refuge Road
Hilton Head Island, SC 29910
Beaufort County
fws.gov/refuge/pinckney_island

Bird lovers rejoice when visiting Pinckney Island National Wildlife Refuge, a 4,000-acre refuge located just off Hilton Head Island. Migrating birds enjoy the safe nesting grounds provided by the sheltered island, which is protected from storms by Hilton Head Island.

TO DO: 🚶 🛶 🎣 🔭 📷 🚴 **FEE: NO**

In the 1800s Charles Cotesworth Pinckney owned a cotton plantation on what is now Pinckney refuge. The land subsequently was used for private hunting excursions until it became part of the Savannah Coastal Refuges Complex in 1975 and was designated Pinckney Island National Refuge. The refuge comprises five large islands and several smaller, unnamed islands. Pinckney Island, the largest island, is the only one with public access, although several of the smaller islands are visible from its trails. The salt marsh ecosystem dominates this picturesque refuge.

There is only one parking area, which is located near the front of the property. From there, visitors can follow the main trail inland, a wide, gravel path that passes Mackay Creek on the right. The trail skirts salt marshes and hardwood forests. Other paths branch out from the main trail, resulting in more than 10 miles of trails throughout the property. The main road is popular with joggers because of its vistas, flat terrain, and wide path.

Hardwood forests, salt marshes, and freshwater ponds surrounded by grassy fields provide homes for the many animals that live on the island, including fox squirrels, white-tailed deer, crabs, and armadillos. Fiddler crabs flit between the spartina and sea oxeye that make up the salt marsh, which is bordered by cabbage palms, live oaks festooned with Spanish moss, and pine trees.

Just 0.7 miles from the parking lot, visitors will encounter Ibis Pond, a small freshwater pond with a patch of land referred to as Bird Island in its center. It is a short walk, and it is one of the most amazing gems of Pinckney. Hundreds of birds nest deep within the thicket of trees and bushes of Bird Island, creating a loud and vibrant rookery. Roseate spoonbills, white ibises, snowy egrets, and tricolored herons often nest here in the spring and summer months. Lucky visitors may spot a great egret guarding her fuzzy, gray chicks. It is rare to see so many large coastal birds nesting in such close proximity as most rookeries are protected from public access. From Ibis Pond, visitors should take a short walk around the entire pond where adult and juvenile alligators like to hang out.

Shorebirds such as piping plovers and seagulls also live in the park; additionally, raptors such as osprey glide above. There are several osprey nests in the park. Painted buntings with bright feathers of blue, orange, yellow, green, and red are frequent visitors to

Wildflowers persist despite Pinckney's poor soil, due largely to its temperate climate.

the park during the spring and summer months. These migrating birds are as colorful as parakeets and thrive in South Carolina's Coastal Plain, residing primarily where forests meet grassy fields. Wood ducks live on the many freshwater ponds sprinkled throughout the island, and the refuge has constructed boxes for nesting pairs. Our national bird, the bald eagle, also nests on the island, although he is more elusive than the aforementioned birds. The large variety and concentration of birds make Pinckney Island National Wildlife Refuge a birding paradise that even non-birders will find intriguing.

While no pets or motorized vehicles are allowed on the island, popular activities include biking, hiking, and kayaking. Biking is a great way to explore the whole island in one day, as walking from one end to the other is quite an undertaking. There is no fee to access the refuge, and there are no facilities on the island, so bring drinking water and use the bathroom before arriving.

Shell Point and Bull Point are short hikes, less than a mile each, that split off from the main road and take visitors out to peninsulas that overlook the Intracoastal Waterway. From these points, it is possible to see the marinas of Hilton Head. Another peninsula provides access to Dick Point Pond, which is on the

GOOD TO KNOW

NEARBY ATTRACTIONS:

Sea Pines Forest Preserve is a small preserve on Hilton Head Island with an Indian shell ring, a meadow that teems with birds and wildflowers, and wetland areas.

Newhall Audubon Nature Preserve on Hilton Head Island offers trails through a variety of habitats, including a small bog and a forest of palms and pines. The type of bog in this preserve, referred to by the Native American word "pocosin," was once a common feature on barrier islands, but due to human activity, is now rare.

OPTIMAL TIME TO VISIT:

In the fall or spring to take advantage of migratory and nesting bird populations.

WHAT'S UNUSUAL:

The opportunity to see rookeries.

BRING:

Binoculars, a bike, and water.

Herons, egrets and other coastal birds dominate the landscape at Pinckney.

opposite side of island and delivers views of neighboring Little Harry Island, Big Harry Island, and Buzzard Island, which are part of the wildlife refuge but not accessible to the public. White Point is another lookout on the far end of the island that gazes over the Port Royal Sound and nearby Corn Island, also a closed-off portion of the refuge.

Near Osprey Pond is a small butterfly garden that attracts many varieties of butterflies easily identifiable through the signs posted outside of their habitat. Also frequent are descriptive plaques that dot the pathways throughout the refuge, detailing the local flora and fauna.

Pinckney is a part of the Savannah Coastal Refuges Complex, and standard refuge rules are in place. Fishing and motorized vehicles are not permitted on the island; however, fishing is permitted in the waterways surrounding the island. In addition, the refuge organizes a deer hunt one day out of the year in order to ensure population control.

This refuge truly represents a quintessential coastal island habitat with its salt marshes, hardwood forest, live oaks draped in Spanish moss, and abundant animal life. This beautiful coastal property, once a cotton plantation, is rich with history, but it has been reclaimed by alligators, crabs, and birds that now thrive among the native plants. It is a calm respite from South Carolina's busy coastal cities.

POINSETT STATE PARK

6660 Poinsett Park Road
Wedgefield, SC 29168
Sumter County
southcarolinaparks.com/poinsett

South Carolina has five distinctive ecoregions based on elevation and location, all of which contain specific plants and animals best suited to their habitats. Poinsett State Park offers the unique ability to sample ecosystems from four of these zones due to its unusual position and topography. Within several walkable miles, hikers view swampy lowland areas, traverse Sandhills pine forests, and then climb bluffs where mountain laurel and rhododendron bloom.

TO DO: 🚶 ⛺ 🎣 🛶 🏊 👓 📷 📖 🚴 🏠 **FEE: YES**

Visitors can see elements of these ecosystems throughout the park. Seashell-embedded stones, a testimony to the now receded beaches that covered the mid-section of the state 50 million years ago, were used as a building material in most of the park's many buildings. The swampy area, which today is below sea level, is indicative of the Lowcountry with its soft, peaty trails and accompanying wildlife. The loblolly and longleaf pine and hardwood forests are barely above sea level and reflect the mid-state's Sandhills topography, while the rolling hills and accompanying mountain laurel show off elements of the Piedmont region.

Technically, Poinsett is located in the northwestern edge of the Coastal Plain of the state, but it does abut the Sandhills zone. Elevation changes are incredibly rare for this region, yet Poinsett is known as the "Mountains of the Midlands" because it rises 220 feet above sea level within the 1,000 acres that make up the park. With the close proximity of these zones, there is obvious overlap and blending. Spanish moss, which prefers to wave peacefully from live oak trees, here decorates mountain laurel bushes. Wildflowers from both the Piedmont and Blue Ridge zones bloom not far from bald cypress knees, enough to confuse any classically trained naturalist.

The park is named for Joel Roberts Poinsett, the South Carolina native who popularized the poinsettia in the United States. It is situated between Columbia and Manning in the center of the state, and was built by the Civilian Conservation Corps (CCC), a New Deal program instituted during the Great Depression to provide work for single, unemployed men. As with other state parks developed by the CCC, there was an emphasis on utilizing local resources. The entrance gates and bathhouse are constructed from the unusual coquina stone, which was quarried on site. Coquina is a sedimentary limestone rock that is made from sand and shells that have fused together, creating a relatively soft material much more common in Florida than South Carolina. It is rarely seen so far inland, and it is interesting to peer at the stones to see seashell fragments.

Lounge chairs and picnic tables conveniently situated in front of the visitors' center invite guests to overlook the 10-acre lake at the center of the park, providing an excellent place to relax on a sunny day. Alligators live year-round in the lake but are rarely spotted and should not be of concern. Fishing

Water lilies provide protection for bullfrog tadpoles, but not for the alligators that frequent the lake.

and non-motorized boat rentals are available, offering a chance to enjoy the lake firsthand. In the spring and early summer, it is worth looking for the river frog and/or tadpole, rare this far north. The large tadpoles have bodies that are nearly as wide as they are long and are about the size of a half dollar. The tadpoles appear in great numbers at the lake's edge, probably attempting to hide from the largemouth bass that live in the deeper areas of the lake.

Also near the visitors' center are the remains of an old grist mill that dates back to pre-Revolutionary times. The Singleton family constructed the mill at the lake's spillway, where the ruins, including the original grinding stone, can still be found. It is said that American Patriots met here to discuss war plans. The CCC purposefully retained these ruins and converted this area into waterfalls that drop between five and seven feet, reminiscent of the upstate's plentiful falls.

Native azaleas are found throughout Poinsett, known as the Mountains of the Midlands for its unusual topography.

For those interested in hiking, Poinsett has a variety of trails that traverse the many ecosystems of the park. Several loop trails, the longest of which is only 2.5 miles, transport visitors from the pine woodlands of the Sandhills region, into bottomland forests reminiscent of the coast and finally through upland forests. It is easy to link these trails together for a longer hike of more than nine miles. For the more enthusiastic hiker, there is also the opportunity to hike into the adjacent 28,000-acre Manchester State Forest. Paths between these two natural areas meet up, allowing hikers to easily utilize both. The Palmetto Trail, which overlaps the park's Coquina Trail, also runs through the two parks.

Most of the trails are fairly flat and easy. The soil underneath one's feet transforms as quickly as the flora in Poinsett, changing from soggy peat bogs that necessitate boardwalks, into sand or compacted dirt. Throughout the park, Spanish moss waves serenely in the breeze from live and deciduous oak, loblolly and longleaf pines, cypress, sweetgum, and a variety of other trees. More than 65 trees have been found in the park's borders, and naturalists also have identified more than 300 species of flowering plants in the park, among them a profusion of wildflowers that bloom in the spring.

A plethora of other plants greets visitors from the side of the trails: mountain laurel, Adam's needle yucca, resurrection fern, American holly, wild ginger, and wax myrtle, to name a few. A variety of birds can be heard singing from trees, and visitors should also look out for red-bellied woodpeckers, red-tailed hawks, and belted kingfishers. In the evenings, Rafinesque big-eared bats may emerge from tree cavities.

Biking is another draw in the park. Biking and horseback riding are allowed in Manchester State Forest, but inexpensive permits may be required. If fishing is a favorite activity, largemouth bass and bream are plentiful in the lake. Mosquito fish, which relish the insect after which they are named, also are abundant and can be discerned by their upside-down mouth that allows them to skim the lake surface in search of a meal.

There are five CCC cabins in the park, available for rent year-round. The cabins have fireplaces and other features constructed of coquina stone, as well as porches and outdoor seating areas.

Poinsett State Park is a great introduction to South Carolina's varying topography or just a worthwhile escape on a weekend. Here it is possible to walk in the tracks of Revolutionary War General Francis Marion, known as the Swamp Fox, or to imagine South Carolinians who lived here and yearned for freedom from Great Britain. It is unique to experience a park with as much history as diversity.

GOOD TO KNOW

NEARBY ATTRACTIONS:
Manchester State Forest is situated adjacent to the park and has great hiking and biking trails. The trails from Poinsett and Manchester State Forest are connected to allow hikers to continue into Manchester State Forest if interested in a longer hike.

Swan Lake Iris Gardens in Sumter, approximately 30 minutes away, is the only American park to feature all eight species of swans. The gardens feature traditional southern gardens, a large pond that brims with irises in May, and an adjacent cypress swamp with an elevated boardwalk.

OPTIMAL TIME TO VISIT:
Spring offers a variety of blooming flowers and other plants, as well as the chance to see large river frog tadpoles. Summer makes for ideal boating and fishing.

WHAT'S UNUSUAL:
The varying topographies in this 1,000-acre park intertwine the normally distinct ecosystems from the Piedmont, Sandhills and coastal regions of the state.

BRING:
Water, and a bike or a horse, if desired.

SANTEE NATIONAL WILDLIFE REFUGE

2125 Fort Watson Road
Summerton, SC
Clarendon County 29148
fws.gov/refuge/santee

With 13,000 acres that range from alligator-filled wetlands to mixed hardwood forests, Santee National Wildlife Refuge has a variety of ecosystems to satisfy everyone from the school child to the avid birder. Due to its sheer magnitude, it can appear overwhelming, but seeing much of what the refuge offers is feasible even in a one-day trip.

TO DO: 🚶 🛶 🎣 👓 📷 📖 🚴 **FEE: NO**

The refuge was established in 1941 to alleviate the loss of wildlife following the construction of two hydroelectric projects on the Santee and Cooper rivers. It sits on the north shore of Lake Marion, the largest lake in South Carolina. With its hardwood and maritime forests, freshwater marshes, cypress swamps, croplands, and managed impoundments, Santee refuge has since become a haven for waterfowl and wildlife. The refuge is home to nearly 300 species of birds, 35 different mammals, and 89 species of reptiles and amphibians, according to the U.S. Fish and Wildlife Service. Depending on the timing of your visit, you are likely to spot osprey, bald eagles, alligators, or wild turkeys, as well as songbirds and waterfowl.

The refuge is divided into four separate sites, some of which are 20 minutes apart from each other. Within the refuge, there are miles of roadways that allow for a variety of wildlife viewing. Foot and canoe paths also are available, but paddling enthusiasts must bring their own craft. The area is flat and easily traversed, although insect spray is recommended.

A good place to begin is at the visitors' center, which has a wealth of information about the area, maps, and explicit directions to the four separate sites, and the only restrooms at the refuge. The center also loans out binoculars along with backpacks that are equipped with field guides.

Just a stone's throw away from this building is the Bluff Unit, which contains a 1,000-year-old Santee Indian mound that was used ceremonially by Native Americans. This is the largest such mound ever discovered on South Carolina's Coastal Plain. Archaeologists have excavated portions, finding graves, pottery shards, and other artifacts. During the Revolutionary War, British troops erected Fort Watson on top of the mound, taking advantage of its height to see great distances. Today, it is accessible by stairs and offers a platform that overlooks both the lake and the top of the dense, nearly impenetrable forest. From here, it is often possible to see an osprey catching its dinner—and possibly even a bald eagle stealing it!

Nearby, the one-mile Wright's Bluff Trail gives visitors the chance to spy songbirds and waterfowl in addition to small mammals. One of South Carolina's most exquisite migratory birds—the painted bunting—is commonly seen here in the spring and summer months. The male painted bunting showcases

British troops erected Fort Watson atop an ancient Indian burial mound that is still preserved at the refuge.

a rainbow of colors, with a blue head, yellow and green back, and bright red belly.

Although only a mile in length, the flat trail traverses a pine and hardwood forest and a floodplain that is waterlogged during spring and early summer. The area is often closed during winter months to protect migratory birds.

Adjacent to this area is Dingle's Pond, a bit of a misnomer as the "pond" is actually a Carolina bay: a natural, oval depression that has filled with water and become a successful wildlife habitat. (For more about the mysterious Carolina bays, see page 164 describing Woods Bay State Park.) Dingle's Pond also has a short trail, about one mile long, and an observation tower where wildlife such as songbirds and wetland birds can be seen. Dingle's Pond is open year-round.

On the other side of the refuge lie the Cuddo and Pine Island units, which

are favored by visitors for their great diversity of habitats. Both have a variety of ponds and swamps as well as managed lands and forests that attract many different birds and animals. These units are a few miles from the visitors' center, but a trip to the Santee refuge would not be complete without seeing one or the other.

At Cuddo, a 7.5-mile drive encircles the unit, bringing visitors through the densely-populated "alligator alley" and other viewing areas. It's a great opportunity to see wildlife in a natural setting for those less inclined to walk, and the road gives visitors a good overview of various habitats. In warmer months, alligators, egrets, herons, and other animals are plentiful along the route, and it is not unusual to see feral pig families; however, late summer can bring low water levels to the area and the wildlife is not as abundant. There are an additional 13.5 miles of hiking trails and dirt roads that come off the main drive. Moreover, paddlers are welcome to utilize another eight miles of canoe and kayak trails that run through the Cuddo unit. Bikes are also welcome on all trails and provide another great way to see the area. This area is generally open year-round.

Pine Island does not permit motorized transportation, but hikers, cyclists, and paddlers are all welcome from March until the end of October. Fishing is also permitted with a valid license. The area is similar to Cuddo in its waterways, wetlands, and forests. Comparable animals also may be seen here, particularly marsh birds such as least bitterns and purple gallinules.

While spring brings great migrations of birds to South Carolina's coastal areas, winter also will deliver great sights. At the Santee refuge, it is possible to find wood ducks, shovelers, sandhill cranes, and many other waterfowl. The gators, however, will likely be staying warm in a semi-hibernated state during the colder months.

Take refuge from the ordinary by visiting this expansive resource. With its plethora of habitats, there is always a good assortment of birds and other animals during the spring and summer months and many intriguing waterfowl during the winter. Bring a good pair of binoculars and a camera to catch the abundant wildlife at Santee.

GOOD TO KNOW

NEARBY ATTRACTIONS:
Super-Sod Farm, at 3086 Five Chop Road in Orangeburg, is regaled by birders for attracting large numbers of birds in the fall after heavy rains.

Santee State Park (page 156)

OPTIMAL TIME TO VISIT:
Spring and early summer to view alligators and the variety of migratory songbirds (though extensive heat or drought reduces the chances of seeing this wildlife); in the winter to see migratory waterfowl.

WHAT'S UNUSUAL:
South Carolina's largest Indian mound, constructed about 1,000 years ago; a variety of habitats ranging from swamps and floodplains to maritime forests and managed impoundments.

BRING:
Bug spray, binoculars, a camera, and a kayak.

SANTEE STATE PARK

251 State Park Road
Santee, SC 29142
Orangeburg County
southcarolinaparks.com/santee

It's often the unusually large fish pulled from Lake Marion that
draw attention to Santee State Park, but with limestone sinkholes,
a cypress forest that looms mysteriously offshore, and a variety of
interesting animals, the park has more to offer than a fish tale.

TO DO: 🚶 ⛺ 🎣 🛶 🏊 🔭 📷 🏠 🚴   **FEE: YES**

One of the best ways to visit the park is by staying in one of the 10 rounded cabins built on piers. Visitors can take in the interesting wildlife and beautiful views by relaxing on the docks that surround the cabins. Santee has 20 other two-bedroom cabins, all with modern facilities, available along the lakeshore, as well as a host of campsites, if the pier cabins aren't available.

The park sits on Lake Marion, the state's largest lake, which was created in the 1940s when the Santee River was dammed for hydroelectric power. The Depression-era project was the largest New Deal project in the state and one of the largest in the country, bringing jobs as well as electricity to many rural South Carolinians. Because the 110,000-acre area was flooded without clearing the land first, underwater cypress trees still exist throughout the lake. Some felled cypress trees, which are slow to rot, have floated to the surface and created "islands" that are beginning to vegetate.

Adjacent to Lake Marion, and connected to it by a canal, is Lake Moultrie. Most boaters prefer Lake Moultrie as it is deeper, has more open areas, and lacks many of the stumps that are the bane of boaters on Lake Marion.

Without a boat, it is difficult to see all that Lake Marion has to offer. If you lack your own craft, one of the best ways to get an overview is through a two-hour boat tour offered by the privately-owned Fisheagle Tours adjacent to the park offices. The tour typically concentrates on the cypress groves and their swamp-like atmosphere where osprey, anhinga, and other wildlife thrive. The alligators, while present in the lake, tend to shy away from human contact, but it is common, except perhaps in the dead of winter, to see several osprey and osprey nests throughout the trip. The guides are generally knowledgeable and informative, and provide information about the history and current environmental conditions of the area. Fisheagle Tours also rents canoes and kayaks to those who prefer to venture out on their own.

For fishermen, Lake Marion is a huge temptation. The lake holds the record for the biggest largemouth bass in South Carolina, a 16.2-pound fish that was pulled from its waters in 1949. Striped bass, white perch, white bass, crappie, channel catfish, and several other varieties of fish are frequently caught in Marion's waters. Catfish are known to thrive at the adjoining Lake Moultrie, and a 136-pound blue catfish was snagged there in 2012. There is no limit on small catfish caught

Spanish moss commonly grows on live oaks but can be found throughout the pine and hardwood forest at Santee State Park.

Lake Marion is a great place for fishing.

Additionally, visitors should be on the lookout for fox squirrels; these are the largest squirrel species in North America, ranging in color from a gray to solid black. Due to their size, they are often mistaken for raccoons. While the animals are intriguing, it is the sinkholes, which can be found in arid, dry areas of the trail, that often draw visitors to the park.

Santee limestone occurs in a narrow belt of the state's Coastal Plain. The limestone was formed millions of years ago when the ocean covered half of what is now South Carolina. Sand and seashells were compacted and transformed into limestone below the surface. Acidic rainwater has permeated through cracks in the limestone, dissolving portions of the rock to form sinkholes and caverns.

The sinkholes can resemble deep holes or pits in the earth. Some fill with water to create ponds during rainy periods. Others remain drier and have caverns that recede deeper in the ground. At least one sinkhole is large enough to fit a house inside. Another drained an entire pond overnight at the park in 1992, while in 2015, extensive flooding caused some sinkholes to collapse and swallow portions of a road. Because the sinkholes appear only to be large holes in the ground, the uninitiated can easily miss them; however, they are interesting geological features that can house

at the lake, although the Department of Natural Resources limits anglers to only one catfish greater than 36 inches per day. Originally, ocean-based striped bass swam in the Santee River, but these fish became landlocked when the river was dammed and their route to the ocean was cut off. They have since thrived in Lake Marion and are a delight to catch at the park.

Off the lake, there also are interesting places to explore. Two trails highlight the park's famous sinkholes, the Limestone and Sinkhole trails, each about a mile long. The Limestone Trail showcases more of the park's wetlands, while the Sinkhole Trail winds through hardwood and pine trees. The forest is a birder's delight, and it is not unusual to see pileated woodpeckers, warblers, tanagers, owls, or turkeys at the park.

different species of salamanders, frogs, snakes, and other animals.

One limestone cavern at Santee is home to a reproductive colony of tri-colored bats, the second smallest bat in the state, weighing less than a quarter of an ounce. While considered common in South Carolina, the Santee colony is the only maternal colony (just mothers and babies; males exist in separate colonies) known in the state, and is thus safeguarded. The area is part of a state Heritage Trust site that protects the caverns, particularly when the bats are nesting or hibernating. However, in September and October, when the bats are neither nesting nor hibernating, rangers sometimes lead interested hikers to the sinkhole when asked.

The park has 10 miles of easy hiking and biking trails. The Sinkhole Trail provides informative signage about sinkholes, but otherwise, hikers must utilize the visitors' center to garner information about animals at the park, as well as its history. Most of the trails are flat as they work their way through the oak and pine forest that dominates this area of the Coastal Plain.

Santee State Park offers both beautiful and unusual landscapes. A visit here should start with a geological history lesson of its limestone substructure, which has done much to influence the plants and animals that live here.

Moving toward the present, visitors can learn about the dam projects that have created new and unusual ecosystems, such as a cypress-filled lake and the presence of non-migrating striped bass. After exploring, a sunset on the lake is a great way to cap off the day; so plan to stay a day or two and take in all this area of the state has to offer.

GOOD TO KNOW

NEARBY ATTRACTIONS:
Lake Moultrie, 30 miles south, is a fisherman's delight. Hikers can enjoy a section of the Palmetto Trail that meanders along the dyke system of the lake.

Santee National Wildlife Refuge (page 152)

Poinsett State Park (page 148)

OPTIMAL TIME TO VISIT:
Spring, summer, and fall to see wildlife. Water level can be low in late summer, which impedes boat travel.

WHAT'S UNUSUAL:
A cypress swamp in the middle of the lake; limestone sinkholes.

BRING:
Camera, bug spray and water.

SAVANNAH NATIONAL WILDLIFE REFUGE

694 Beech Hill Lane
Hardeeville, SC 29927
Jasper County
fws.gov/refuge/savannah

For those who love alligators, Savannah National Wildlife Refuge is a must-see. The refuge has an abundant alligator population due to the large amount of freshwater within its borders. Even on a mild, 65-degree day in early spring, alligators lounge along the shore of the many canals in the refuge, soaking up rays on patches of grass. Gators as large as 10 feet are plentiful, as are their tiny young counterparts who frequently gather in small groups for protection.

TO DO: 🥾 🎣 👓 📷 📖   **FEE: NO**

There are many animals and plants to be found within the roughly 29,000 acres of this refuge. A great place to begin is on the four-mile Wildlife Drive. This drive can take upwards of an hour, as there is so much to see on the way. Be prepared to stop frequently to snap photographs of alligators, ibises, or moorhens. Both glossy and white ibises are year-round visitors to the park. There are plenty of walking paths adjacent to the driving trail, providing an excellent opportunity for visitors to stretch their legs. Examples include the Raccoon Island Trail, the Plantation Island Trail, and the Recess Plantation Trail. Another trail, the short 0.1-mile Cistern Trail leads to a bird blind set out over a pond where visitors can remain unseen to wildlife in the area. Alligators, birds, and small mammals such as raccoons may pass by this box, completely unaware that they are being watched from adjustable blinds. This trail also passes by the remains of an old cistern that was used to collect rainwater.

The longer trails (Raccoon Island, 1.3; Plantation Island Trail, 2.5; Recess Plantation Trail, 3.2) each loop around small ponds, which are excellent opportunities to see wildlife up close. These ponds are remnants of the dike system that was set up in the 1700s when the land was part of a large rice plantation. Large, wooden contraptions called rice trunks control the degree to which water from the Savannah River flows into the refuge. While once used to control the water levels for farming, the trunks are now used to monitor the water levels throughout the refuge, creating environments that are hospitable to wetland bird populations. When driving through the refuge, an AM radio station provides historical information about the refuge's former rice plantation days.

Egrets make a home in Savannah National Wildlife Refuge year-round.

The Savannah National Wildlife Refuge is located on the South Carolina and Georgia border and stretches into both states; however, about 70 percent of its land is in South Carolina. Because the refuge is so southerly, it houses many species not normally seen in South Carolina. One such animal is the purple gallinule, a medium-sized wading bird with bright peacock-like plumage—greens, purples, and blues—and massive, chicken-like, yellow legs. Even their beaks are multicolored, striped with yellow, orange, and cerulean. This bird is one of the main draws of the refuge and is portrayed prominently on its website and within its brochures. See the purple gallinule during its summer nesting season; it is commonly seen between June and August.

Several species of owls also nest within the park. The eastern screech owl, great horned owl, and the barred owl are all commonly sighted year-round. Many ducks, such as wood ducks, are permanent residents in the park, and northern shovelers, with their unique, spoon-like bills, visit the park in the winter. Both are common. This refuge is a prime destination for bird watching, and an incredibly detailed list of the birds is available at the visitors' center or online. The list divides the birds into categories based on their species and details when they visit or nest in the park, as well as how "common" they are.

Other wildlife in the park includes bobcats, raccoons, river otters, and many varieties of snakes. It is unusual to see a bobcat, but the best chance lies on Wildlife Drive, as they are shy and like to keep out of the way of humans; it is easier to sneak up on them when driving on the road than when walking. Look for these aloof creatures perched on tree branches where they sleep during the day.

The scenery in here is stunning. Large ponds dot the refuge, and hammocks—islands of

GOOD TO KNOW

NEARBY ATTRACTIONS:
The **Savannah Refuge Coastal Complex** stretches throughout Georgia, and several of the refuges that make up this complex are nearby, such as the Wassaw National Wildlife Refuge.

OPTIMAL TIME TO VISIT:
Avoid the heat of the summer, but spring and fall will showcase the vast number of alligators here. Winter for migratory waterfowl; spring for other birds.

WHAT'S UNUSUAL:
Visiting a coastal refuge with a large freshwater system; the chance to see a plethora of alligators and rare birds that are seldom seen in South Carolina.

BRING:
Water and binoculars.

trees within grass- or marshlands—are interspersed throughout. Within these hammocks, live oaks are festooned with thick clumps of Spanish moss that create eerie-looking paths.

Most of the refuge is open space—marshes, ponds, grasslands—but Kingfisher Pond provides a very different habitat. A one-mile loop trail takes visitors through a forest teeming with ferns and pines. Although this area is technically a hammock, it is much larger than the hammocks in the remainder of the refuge and thus seems like a small forest. There is a separate parking area for this section of the refuge, but it is also hikeable via the Tupelo Trail, which is roughly 3.4 miles one way.

Savannah National Wildlife Refuge is definitely an outdoor destination that deserves an entire day to explore. Stop by the visitors' center and grab the necessary literature on the refuge, and, if traveling with children, borrow one of the refuge's backpacks filled with binoculars and other gear. Hike along the ponds and next to the canals in the park, keep an eye out for alligators, and take beautiful photographs at this coastal gem.

Spanish moss-laden live oaks line driving routes where visitors can encounter a multitude of American alligators.

WOODS BAY STATE PARK

11020 Woods Bay Rd
Olanta, SC 29114
Florence County
southcarolinaparks.com/woodsbay

Of the great variety of landforms throughout the state, Carolina bays remain one of the greatest enigmas. These once-plentiful, elliptical-shaped depressions occur throughout the Atlantic Coastal Plain, but seem to be most prevalent in the Carolinas. Despite their profusion, scientists remain mystified by their uniformity and presence. Woods Bay State Park contains one of the largest and least-disturbed examples of these inland wonders.

TO DO: 🥾 🎣 🛶 🔭 📷 📖   **FEE: NO**

Carolina bays are not coastal formations but occur inland on the Coastal Plain. The name "Carolina bay" probably derives from the abundance of bay trees that typically surround their perimeter. Most of the 4,000 documented Carolina bays throughout the state are clustered together, often overlapping one another. However, the majority of these bays have been greatly altered by human land use, most commonly for farming. Only about 220 are considered intact and appropriately reminiscent of their natural state, and most of these are still at risk of being lost as they are privately owned.

Carolina bays share many characteristics. All are elliptically shaped with their axes aligned in a northwest to southeast direction. All bays have sand deposits in their southeast and northeast edges. As depressions, they often collect and retain rainwater above the normal water table, and thus support a variety of plant life. Most, however, retain water only seasonally; although a few, such as Woods Bay, remain swampy year-round.

Scientists have had several theories regarding Carolina bay formation. Some once believed they were the scar tissue of a prehistoric meteorite bombardment, accounting for their identical elliptical shapes that point in the same direction. These days, most embrace the theory that millions of years ago receding oceans left behind small bodies of water. Prevailing winds that originated in the southwest created currents that further eroded these ponds, creating the current Carolina bays.

Woods Bay is a great place to see the variety of plants and wildlife that inhabit these natural mysteries. Because Woods Bay is fed by underground springs, it stays wet throughout the seasons. The water is tinted a deep brown due to the wealth of cypress trees that unload tannins into the water. A 1,150-foot boardwalk (which the park plans to expand) allows visitors to appreciate the bay without getting wet feet. The boardwalk meanders through a cypress and tupelo swamp, working its way into a dense shrub bog before it terminates at the edge of the bay where sedge grasses grow. As the boardwalk works its way into the swamp, the foliage of tupelo gum, cypress, water oak, and maple trees shuts out the sky. The transformation from a healthy pine forest into a dense swamp is quick and eerie. The presence of gators further augments this eeriness, even though they are a bit elusive at the park.

Woods Bay remains swampy year-round, allowing bald cypress and swamp tupelo to thrive along its shore.

GOOD TO KNOW

NEARBY ATTRACTIONS:
Lee State Park, about a 50-minute drive, has short hiking and equestrian trails, artesian wells, and a bottomland hardwood forest through which the Lynches River runs.

OPTIMAL TIME TO VISIT:
Spring to see blooms and migratory birds; winter for the most expansive, unobscured views of the bay.

WHAT'S UNUSUAL:
Seeing a well-preserved Carolina bay.

BRING:
Bug spray, water, and a camera.

Also of interest are the carnivorous plants such as sundews, bladderworts, and pitcher plants that grow underneath the boardwalk. Additionally, a wealth of dragonflies reduces mosquito levels, but sightseers should nevertheless come equipped with bug spray.

Until the boardwalk is expanded, the best way to get a closer view of Woods Bay is along the one-mile canoe trail at the park. (Visitors can rent watercraft from the park office.) The canoe trail is accessible most of the year and allows slow passage through a quintessential cypress swamp.

For those spooked by the presence of alligators in the water, there is also another walkable one-mile nature trail that winds its way from the boardwalk entrance to several holding ponds and an old historic millpond. Woods Bay once housed a cotton gin, and in the mid-19th century, it was home to a bay-powered gristmill, part of which is still standing. By the 1930s, this gristmill was laid to rest, and the park was purchased by the state in 1973.

The bay was marginally disturbed when it was logged for cypress in the 1920s. Since that era, however, little has impacted its natural state. Still, the bay has been changed because naturally occurring fires that would normally reduce loblolly pine numbers have been suppressed, allowing these pines to proliferate. As such, loblollies have begun to dominate where the more fire-resistant gum and cypress trees once reigned.

The 1,590-acre park has marshes, sandy soil, an oak-hickory forest, and a shrub bog. It hosts a variety of wildlife, including alligators, carpenter tree frogs, and about 75 other species of animals, including many types of reptiles and amphibians. Birders will especially appreciate the more than 150 varieties that have been documented at Woods Bay. All of these components make for a fragile, strange, and unique habitat deserving of exploration.

A boardwalk allows visitors to venture to the interior of the bay to view wildlife and plants.

NOTES & CITATIONS

PIEDMONT/ MOUNTAINS

Caesars Head State Park

"Caesars Head Hawk Watch." HawkCount. August 1, 2014. Accessed October 28, 2015. http://hawkcount.org/siteinfo. php?rsite=551.

"Caesars Head State Park." Caesars Head State Park. 2015. Accessed October 26, 2015. http://www.southcarolinaparks. com/caesarshead/introduction. aspx

Hendershot, Don. "Watch You like a Hawk." Smoky Mountain Living. July 30, 2015.

Accessed October 28, 2015. http://www.smliv.com/depart- ments/outdoors/watch-you-like- a-hawk/.

Chau Ram County Park

"Chau Ram Park - Oconee County, SC." Experience Oconee. 2015. Accessed October 29, 2015. http://experienceoconee.com/ Parks/Chau-Ram-Park

Lambert, Yon, and Ned Cannon. "Looking for a Nature-based Getaway Right Here in the Upstate? Choose Chau-Ram." GoUpstate.com. July 22, 2004. Accessed October 29, 2015. http://www.goupstate. com/article/20040722/ NEWS/407220311

Molloy, Johnny. "Chauga River Loop at Chau Ram Park." In *Ex- plorer's Guide 50 Hikes in South Carolina: Walks, Hikes & Back- packing*. Woodstock, Vermont: Country Man Press, 2007.

"Oconee CVB Jocassee Gorges Lakes Mountains Rivers and Wa- terfalls." Oconee CVB Jocassee

Gorges Lakes Mountains Rivers and Waterfalls. 2013. Accessed October 29, 2015. http://www.scmountainlakes. com/uploads/experience/water- falls.asp

"Oconee County, SC." USA.com. 2015. Accessed October 29, 2015. http://www.usa.com/oconee- county-sc.htm

Croft State Park

"Camp Croft." Camp Croft. Ac- cessed October 1, 2015. http://campcroft.net/history.aspx

"Croft Passage." Palmetto Trail. Accessed October 28, 2015. http://www.palmettotrail.org/ croftpassage.asp.

"Croft State Park." Croft State Park. 2015. Accessed October 26, 2015. http://southcarolinaparks.com/ croft/introduction.aspdx

"Edwin M. Griffin Nature Pre- serve." SPACE. 2015. Accessed October 28, 2015. http://spartanburgconservation. org/properties/cottonwood-trail/.

"Glendale Shoals Preserve." SPACE. 2015. Accessed October 28, 2015. http://spartanburgconservation. org/properties/cottonwood-trail/.

"Welcome to the Francis Marion and Sumter National Forests!" United States Department of Agriculture. Accessed October 28, 2015. http://www.fs.usda.gov/scnfs.

Devils Fork State Park

"Devils Fork State Park." South Carolina State Parks. Accessed October 24, 2015. http://www.southcarolinaparks. com/devilsfork/introduction.aspx

"Harvard University Herbaria - Bot- any Libraries Archives Asa Gray Bicentennial 1810."

Harvard University Herbaria - Botany Libraries Archives Asa Gray Bi- centennial 1810. Accessed. April 24, 2015. http://botlib.huh.harvard.edu/ libraries/Gray_Bicent/shortia_ galacifolia.html

"Great Lake: Explore Lake Jocassee, One of the Last Great Places." Blue Ridge Outdoors Magazine RSS. June 30, 2013. Accessed April 24, 2015. http://www.blueridgeoutdoors. com/paddling/great-lake-explore- lake-jocassee/

"Waterfall Trail." SCTrails.net. Oc- tober 21, 2005. Accessed October 26, 2015. http://www.sctrails.net/trails/all- trails/waterfalls/laurelfork.html

Connor, Eric. "Bygone World Lies Beneath Jocassee's Surface." Bygone World Lies Beneath Jocassee's Surface. September 6, 2012. Accessed October 26, 2015. http://www.greenvilleon- line.com/article/20120906/ NEWS07/309060007/Bygone- world-lies-beneath-Jocassee-s-sur- face

Forty Acre Rock Heritage Preserve

"Forty Acre Rock." SCIWAY: South Carolina's Information Highway. Accessed October 28, 2015. http:// www.sciway.net/sc-photos/lancast- er-county/forty-acre-rock.html.

Green, Sara. "Foray at Forty Acre Rock." South Carolina Wildlife Federation. Accessed October 28, 2015. http://www.scwf.org/index.php/ events/full-calendar/175-foray-at- forty-acre-rock.

Jones Gap State Park

"Hiking Trail." Hiking Trail. June 26, 2008. Accessed October 28, 2015. http://www.sctrails.net/trails/ alltrails/hiking/upcountry/Hospi- talRock.html.

"Jones Gap State Park." Jones Gap State Park. 2015. Accessed Octo- ber 26, 2015. http://www.southcarolinaparks. com/jonesgap/introduction.aspx

"Middle Saluda River." Scenic River Programs. Accessed October 26, 2015. http://www.dnr.sc.gov/water/envaff/ river/scenic/midsaluda.html.

"Mountain Bridge Wilderness." Hiking the Carolinas. Accessed October 26, 2015. http://hikingthecarolinas.com/ mountain_bridge_wilderness. php.

Keowee Toxaway State Park

"Jocassee Gorges - A Partnership in Conservation." Department of Nat- ural Resources. Accessed October 26, 2015. http://www.dnr.sc.gov/managed/ wild/jocassee/indexfull.htm.

"Keowee Toxaway State Park." Ke- owee Toxaway State Park. 2015. Accessed October 26, 2015. http://southcarolinaparks.com/ keoweetoxaway/introduction.aspx

"Jocassee's Gorges: An Intense Concentration of Waterfalls." *50 of the World's Last Great Places Destinations of a Lifetime*, 2012, 24-27.

Kings Mountain State Park

"Kings Mountain State Park." Kings Mountain State Park. 2015. Ac- cessed October 26, 2015. http://southcarolinaparks.com/ kingsmountain/

"SCDAH." SCDAH. Accessed October 26, 2015. http://www.nationalregister.sc.gov/cherokee/S10817711022/index.htm.

United States. National Park Service. "Kings Mountain National Military Park (U.S. National Park Service)." National Parks Service. October 22, 2015. Accessed October 26, 2015. http://www.nps.gov/kimo/index.htm.

Landsford Canal State Park

Mitchell, Arthur. In *South Carolina Irish*. Charleston, South Carolina: History Press, 2011, page 69.

Porcher, Richard D., and Douglas A. Rayner. *A Guide to the Wildflowers of South Carolina*. Columbia, S.C.: University of South Carolina Press, 2001.

South Carolina Department of Archives and History (SCDAH); Accessed April 23, 2015. http://www.nationalregister.sc.gov/chester/S10817712001/

"South Carolina Parks - South Carolina Parks Official Site." South Carolina Parks - South Carolina Parks Official Site. Accessed October 23, 2015.

Musgrove Mill State Historic Site

"Musgrove Mill State Historic Site." Discover South Carolina. Accessed May 24, 2015. http://www.discovercarolina.com/html/s04history109a.pdf

"Musgrove Mill State Historic Site." South Carolina Parks - South Carolina Parks Official Site. Accessed May 24, 2015. http://www.southcarolinaparks.com/musgrovemill/introduction.aspx

"Horseshoe Falls." SCIWAY: South Carolina's Front Door. Accessed May 24, 2015. http://www.sciway.net/sc-photos/laurens-county/horseshoe-falls.html

Oconee State Park

"Oconee State Park." South Carolina State Parks. 2015. Accessed October 26, 2015. http://southcarolinaparks.com/oconee/introduction.aspx.

"Oconee Station State Historic Site." South Carolina State Parks. 2015. Accessed October 26, 2015. http://southcarolinaparks.com/oconeestation/introduction.aspx

"Foothills Trail Conference." Foothills Trail Conference. 2015. Accessed October 26, 2015. http://www.foothillstrail.org/.

Paris Mountain State Park

Edgar, Walter B. *The South Carolina Encyclopedia*. Columbia, South Carolina: University of South Carolina Press, 2006.

Neely, Kirk. "The Mysteries of Paris Mountain." Kirk H. Neely, Storyteller, Writer, Pastor, Teacher, Counselor, Artist. May 14, 2010. Accessed June 15, 2015. <http://kirkhneely.com/2010/05/14/the-mysteries-of-paris-mountain/

"Paris Mountain State Park." South Carolina State Parks. Accessed June 16, 2015. http://www.southcarolinaparks.com/parismountain/introduction.aspx

Stevens Creek Heritage Preserve

Gelbart, Mark. "The Curious Disjunct Range of the Miccosukee Gooseberry (Ribes Echineiium)." GeorgiaBeforePeople. April 25, 2012. Accessed October 20, 2015.

McMillan, Patrick. "Stevens Creek Heritage Preserve." NameThatPlant.net.: 2002. Accessed October 29, 2015. http://www.namethatplant.net/where_stevenscreek.shtml

Porcher, Richard D., and Douglas A. Rayner. *A Guide to the Wildflowers of South Carolina*. Columbia, S.C.: University of South Carolina Press, 2001.

Stumphouse Mountain Heritage Preserve

"About White-nose Syndrome." White-Nose Syndrome. 2015. Accessed October 26, 2015. https://www.whitenosesyndrome.org/about-white-nose-syndrome

"National Forests in North Carolina - Special Places." USDA Forest Service. 2015. Accessed October 26, 2015. http://www.fs.usda.gov/detail/nfsnc/specialplaces/?cid=stelprdb5188436.

"Stumphouse Tunnel." SCIWAY. 2015. Accessed October 26, 2015. http://www.sciway.net/sc-photos/oconee-county/stumphouse-tunnel.html.

"Stumphouse Tunnel Park and Issaqueena Falls." OoneeCountry. 2015. Accessed October 26, 2015. http://www.oconeecountry.com/stumphouse.html.

"Waterfall Trail." SC Trails. October 25, 2005. Accessed October 26, 2015. http://www.sctrails.net/trails/alltrails/waterfalls/yellowbranch.html.

Table Rock State Park

"GNIS Detail - Pinnacle Mountain." GNIS Detail - Pinnacle Mountain. Accessed October 1, 2015. http://geonames.usgs.gov/apex/f?p=gnispq:3:0::NO::P3_FID:1225507

"Introduction." *Table Rock State Park*. South Carolina State Park, 2015. Web. 25 Oct. 2015. http://www.southcarolinaparks.com/tablerock/introduction.aspx

"Roper House Complex, Pickens County, SC." Roper House Complex, Pickens County, SC. Accessed October 1, 2015. http://www.nationalregister.sc.gov/pickens/S10817739018/

THE SANDHILLS

Aiken State Park

"Aiken State Park." South Carolina State Parks. Accessed October 29, 2015. http://southcarolinaparks.com/aiken/introduction.aspx.

"The Edisto River." Friends of the Edisto. December 2, 2014. Accessed October 29, 2015. http://www.edistofriends.org/edisto-river.

Carolina Sandhills National Wildlife Refuge

"Carolina Sandhills National Wildlife Refuge." Carolina Sandhills National Wildlife Refuge. 2007. Accessed April 27, 2015.

Carolina Sandhllls National Wildlife Refuge (brochure), U.S. Fish and Wildlife Service, September 2007. http://www.fws.gov/carolinasandhills/

Finch, Bill. *Longleaf, Far as the Eye Can See: A New Vision of North America's Richest Forest*. Chapel Hill, North Carolina: University of North Carolina Press, 2012.

Cheraw State Park

Earley, Lawrence S. *Looking for Longleaf: The Fall and Rise of an American Forest*. Chapel Hill, North Carolina: University of North Carolina Press, 2004.

"Long-Leaf Pine Range Conservation Initiative." October 1, 2009. Accessed April 27, 2015. http://www.fws.gov/southeast/shc/pdf/LongleafPineLCC. pdf

Porcher, Richard, and Douglas Rayner. *A Guide to the Wildflowers of South Carolina*. Columbia, SC: University of South Carolina Press, 2001. 436-439.

"South Carolina Parks - South Carolina Parks Official Site." South Carolina Parks - South Carolina Parks Official Site. Accessed December 30, 2014

Goodale State Park

Foster, Caroline. "N. R. Goodale State Park by Caroline Foster." SC Wildlife Magazine. Mar/Apr 2006 Accessed October 29, 2015. http://www.scwildlife.com/articles/marapril2006/NRGoodaleStatePark.html

"Goodale State Park." South Carolina State Parks. Accessed October 29, 2015. http://southcarolinaparks.com/goodale/introduction.aspx

"Hades the Greek God of the Underworld." Greek Myths and Greek Mythology. Accessed October 29, 2015. http://www.greekmyths-greek-mythology.com/hades-greek-god-underworld/

Hitchcock Woods

Fraker, Julia. "10 Terrific Thanksgiving Traditions around the Country." The Huffington Post. 2010. Accessed April 27, 2015.

www.huffingtonpost.com/2010/11/25/thanksgiving-2010-traditions_n_787935.html

"Hitchcock Woods Foundation." Hitchcock Woods Foundation. 2015. Accessed October 28, 2015. http://www.hitchcockwoods.org/

Shealy, Harry. "What Makes Hitchcock Woods Special to Me." Hitchcock Woods Foundation. Accessed October 27, 2015. http://www.hitchcockwoods.org/media/articles/2010/AHS2010_Special.pdf

Bear and Donnelly Islands

"ACE Basin Project Celebrates 25 Years of Land Conservation." ACE Basin. Accessed August 9, 2015.

"Protecting South Carolina's ACE Basin | The Nature Conservancy." Protecting South Carolina's ACE Basin | The Nature Conservancy. Accessed April 10, 2015.

U.S. Fish and Wildlife Service, Ernest F. Hollings ACE Basin, Accessed August, 2015.

COASTAL PLAIN/ COASTAL ZONE

Botany Bay Heritage Preserve

"Botany Bay Plantation Heritage Preserve/Wildlife Management Area." SCDNR Managed Lands. 2007. Accessed October 28, 2015. https://www.dnr.sc.gov/mlands/managedland?p_id=57.

"Roxbury Park." Town of Meggett's Roxbury Park. Accessed October 28, 2015. http://www.roxburypark.org/.

Bulls Island

Clark, John F., and John Dantzler. "Bulls Island." In *Hiking South Carolina*. Helena, Mont.: Falcon, 1998, page 201.

Conner, William H., W. David Mixon, and Gene W. Wood. "Maritime Forest Habitat Dynamics on Bulls Island, Cape Romain National Wildlife Refuge, SC, following Hurricane Hugo." *Forest Ecology and Management* 212, no. 1-3 (2005): 127-34.

Dixon, Chris. "Tracking 'Alligatorzilla': Gator Is Huge — and Possibly Bashful." *The (Charleston) Post and Courier*, January 16, 2006, Nation sec.

Haar, Carolyn. "Bulls Island." *Island Magazine*, 2014, 4-9. http:/www.palmtreepublishing.net/.../islandmagazine_2014.../d7851fe44f.pdf

"Red Wolves - Cape Romain - U.S. Fish and Wildlife Service." Red Wolves - Cape Romain - U.S. Fish and Wildlife Service. Accessed March 26, 2015. http:/www.fws.gov/refuge/Cape_Romain/wildlife_and_habitat/red_wolves.html

Caw Caw Interpretive Center

"Caw Caw Interpretive Center." Charleston County Parks and Recreation. Accessed October 28, 2015. http://www.ccprc.com/53/Caw-Caw-Interpretive-Center.

Congaree National Park

Bronaugh, Whit. "Congaree: Where the Trees Are Still Tall - American Forests." American Forests. 2009. Accessed April 27, 2015. http://www.americanforests.org/magazine/article/congaree-where-the-trees-are-still-tall/

"Congaree National Park." National Parks Service. October 14, 2015. Accessed October 27, 2015. http://www.nps.gov/cong/index.htm

Gaddy, L. L., and John Emmett Cely. "Life in the Swamp." In *The Natural History of Congaree*

Swamp. Manning, South Carolina: Published for Terra Incognita Books by Totally Outdoors Imaging, 2012.

Holleman, Joey. "Synchronized Fireflies Putting on a Show at Congaree Park." *The (Columbia) State Newspaper*, June 4, 2014. http://www.thestate.com/living/article13858442.html

"Wilderness.net - Congaree National Park Wilderness - General Information." Wilderness.net. Accessed April 27, 2015. http://www.wilderness.net/NWPS/wildView?WID134

Edisto Beach State Park

"Land Trust History." Edisto Island Open Land Trust, Preservation, Protection, Easement. Accessed April 10, 2015.

Mitchel, Liz. "Loggerheads Nesting in Big Numbers." *The Charlotte Observer*, Charlotte, NC. August 21, 2008.

Francis Beidler Forest

"Francis Beidler Forest." NPS: Explore Nature » NNL » Sites. Accessed October 1, 2015. http://www.nature.nps.gov/nnl/site.cfm?Site=FRBE-SC

"Beidler Forest | Audubon." Beidler Forest | Audubon. Accessed October 1, 2015. http://beidlerforest.audubon.org/

"Introduction." Givhans Ferry State Park Cabins. Accessed October 1, 2015. http://southcarolinaparks.com/givhansferry/introduction.aspx

Hunting Island State Park

"Hunting Island State Park." Hunting Island State Park. 2015. Accessed October 26, 2015. http://southcarolinaparks.com/huntingisland/introduction.aspdx

Huntington Beach State Park

"Huntington Beach State Park." Huntington Beach State Park. 2015. Accessed October 26, 2015. http://southcarolinaparks.com/huntingtonbeach/introduction.aspx

Lewis Ocean Bay Heritage Preserve

"Lewis Ocean Bay." Department of Natural Resources. Accessed October 26, 2015. https://www.dnr.sc.gov/mlands/directions?p_id=104.

Lighthouse Inlet Heritage Preserve "~ Brief History ~." SaveTheLight.org. Accessed October 26, 2015. http://www.savethelight.org/briefhistory.html.

"Lighthouse Inlet Heritage Preserve." Department of Natural Resources. Accessed October 26, 2015. https://www.dnr.sc.gov/mlands/managedland?p_id=26.

"Morris Island Lighthouse." LighthouseFriends. Accessed October 26, 2015. http://www.lighthousefriends.com/light.asp?ID=333.

Peach Tree Rock Heritage Preserve

Kowtko, Stacy. *America's Natural Places: South and Southwest.* Santa Barbara, CA: ABC-CLIO, LLC, 2010. 120-121.

"Peachtree Rock Heritage Preserve | The Nature Conservancy." Peachtree Rock Heritage Preserve | The Nature Conservancy. Accessed December 30, 2014. http://www.nature.org/ourinitiatives/regions/northamerica/unitedstates/southcarolina/placesweprotect/peachtree-rock-heritage-preserve.xml

"Peachtree Rock Nature Preserve." South Carolina State Trails Program. August 1, 2008. Accessed October 28, 2015.

http://www.sctrails.net/trails/alltrails/hiking/midlands/peachtreerock.html

"South Carolina Department of Natural Resources." SCDNR. Accessed December 30, 2014. http://www.dnr.sc.gov/mlands/hpprogram.html.

"South Carolina Department of Natural Resources." SCDNR. 2014. Accessed October 28, 2015. http://www.dnr.sc.gov/mlands/hpprogram.html.

Pinckney National Wildlife Refuge

"Pinckney Island - U.S. Fish and Wildlife Service." Pinckney Island - U.S. Fish and Wildlife Service. October 22, 2015. Accessed October 26, 2015. http://www.fws.gov/refuge/Pinckney_Island/.

"Pinckney Island National Wildlife Refuge." Pinckney Island National Wildlife Refuge. Accessed October 26, 2015. http://www.fws.gov/refuges/profiles/index.cfm?id=41629.

Poinsett State Park

Anderson, Amber; Don, Jacqueline, Johnston, Taylor; and Sanders, Sarah. "American Historic Landscape Poinsett State Park" pdf April 3, 2014; Accessed Oct. 28, 2015. http://www.clemson.edu/caah/.../poinsett-state-park.pdf

Angel, Robert. "Mobile Studio Travels of the Carolina Considered Project.": Poinsett State Park, South Carolina. Part I. Drive Over and Entrance Gate. May 10, 2010. Accessed October 28, 2015. http://mobilestudiotravels.blogspot.com/2010/05/poinsett-state-park-south-carolina-part.html.

"Habitats, Plants and Animals of Poinsett State Park." South Carolina State Parks. 2009.

Accessed October 28, 2015. http://www.southcarolinaparks.com/.../State Parks Files/Poinsett/PO_hp...

"Manchester State Forest." South Carolina Forestry Commission. Accessed October 28, 2015. http://www.state.sc.us/forest/refman.htm.

"Poinsett State Park." South Carolina State Parks. Accessed October 28, 2015. http://southcarolinaparks.com/poinsett/introduction.aspx.

"Swan Lake Iris Gardens - City of Sumter, SC." Swan Lake Iris Gardens - City of Sumter, SC. Accessed October 28, 2015. http://www.sumtersc.gov/swan-lake-iris-gardens.aspx.

Santee National Wildlife Refuge

Robin, Carter. "Carolina Bird Club." Carolina Bird Club. Accessed October 16, 2015. http://www.carolinabirdclub.org/sites/SC/santee_nwr.html

"Santee National Wildlife Refuge." Santee National Wildlife Refuge. Accessed October 28, 2015. http://www.fws.gov/refuges/profiles/index.cfm?id=42570

"Visitor Activities - Santee - U.S. Fish and Wildlife Service." Visitor Activities - Santee - U.S. Fish and Wildlife Service. August 8, 2015. Accessed October 28, 2015. http://www.fws.gov/refuge/Santee/visit/visitor_activities.html

Santee State Park

In Search of Sinkholes, *The Times and Democrat*, Orangeburg, SC, Oct. 16, 2005 http://thetandd.com/news/in-search-of-sinkholes-santee-state-park-s-limestone-deposits/article_b45df3a2-8310-52cd-9ef9-063f17c063ca.html

Santee Jungle Guide, Santee Cooper Catfish Guides, Accessed October 24, 2014. http://www.santeecajunguide.com/contact.html

"Santee State Park." South Carolina Parks - South Carolina Parks Official Site. Accessed October 24, 2015. http://www.southcarolinaparks.com/santee/introduction.aspx

South Carolina, A History, by Walter Edgar, University of South Carolina Press, 1998. Page 503.

Savannah National Wildlife Refuge

"Savannah - U.S. Fish and Wildlife Service." Savannah - U.S. Fish and Wildlife Service. October 16, 2015. Accessed October 26, 2015. http://www.fws.gov/refuge/savannah/.

Woods Bay State Park

Bennett, Steven, and John Nelson. "Distribution of Carolina Bays in South Carolina." 1991. Accessed October 28, 2015. http://www.scstatehouse.gov/.../IsolatedWetlandsandCarolinaBaysTaskForce/.../...

Porcher, Richard D., and Douglas A. Rayner. "Carolina Bays and the Coastal Plain." In *A Guide to the Wildflowers of South Carolina*. Columbia, SC: University of South Carolina Press, 2001.

"Introduction." Woods Bay State Park Located in Olanta, SC. Accessed October 28, 2015. http://southcarolinaparks.com/woods-bay/introduction.aspx.

Stewart, Kevin G., and Mary Roberson. *Exploring the Geology of the Carolinas: A Field Guide to Favorite Places from Chimney Rock to Charleston*. Chapel Hill, North Carolina: University of North Carolina Press, 2007.

DONORS

THE HUB CITY WRITERS PROJECT THANKS ITS FRIENDS WHO MADE CONTRIBUTIONS IN SUPPORT OF THIS BOOK AND OTHER HUB CITY PROGRAMS.

Randall and Sally
Chambers
Sarah Chambers and
Becky Pennell
Elizabeth Chapman
Norman and Muffet
Chapman
Robert H. and Lacy
Chapman III
Bill Chidester
Robert and Janeen
Cochran
Rick and Sue Conner
Patricia and Joe Cornwell
Tom Moore Craig
John and Kirsten Cribb
Nancy Rainey Crowley
Betsy Cox and Mike Curtis
J.K. Daniels
Kate and John Dargan
Kenneth and Rachel
Deems
Carolyn Dempsey
Frederick Dent
Magruder H. Dent
Chris and Alice Dorrance
Jean Dunbar
Coleman Edmunds
William C. and Betty
Elston
Ed and Carol Eppes
Wallace Eppes
Lyssa and Eric Foust
Julia Franks
Elaine T. Freeman
Barney and Elaine Gosnell
Andrew Green
Margaret and Chip Green
Suzannah and Scott Griffin
John Morton and Susan
Griswold
Jim and Kay Gross
Roger and Marianna
Habisreutinger
Lee and Kitty Hagglund
Benjy and Tanya Hamm
Al and Anita Hammerbeck
Bob and Barbara Hammett
Monty and Julian Hankinson

Tom and Tracy Hannah
Robert and Carolyn
Harbison, III
John and Lou Ann Harrill, Jr.
Peyton and Michele Harvey
Jonathan Haupt
Mark Hayes
David and Rita Heatherly
Rebecca and Steve
Hedges
Gary and Carmela
Henderson
Elaine Hester
Stephanie Highsmith
Ralph and Susan Hilsman
Charlie Hodge
Marion Peter Holt
Myrta and David Holt
Doug and Marilyn Hubbell
Josephine Hutcheson
Max Hyde
Gerada Hyder
Susan Hodge Irwin
Sadie Jackson
Steve and Melissa Johnson
Stewart and Ann Johnson
Wallace Eppes Johnson
Betsy and Charles Jones
Frannie Jordan
Daniel Kahrs
Jay and Pam Kaplan
Nancy Zoole Kenney
Thomas and Mary Killoren
Wendy and Dan King
Bert and Ruth Knight
Mr. and Mrs. John M.
Kohler, Jr.
Connie McCarley Kunak
Mary Jane and Cecil
Lanford
Jack and Kay Lawrence
Eric and Brandy Lindsey
George and Frances
Loudon
Brownlee and Julie Lowry
Gayle Magruder
Kari and Phillip Mailloux
Nancy Mandlove
Bill and Wendy Mayrose

John and Stacy McBride
Fayssoux McLean
James McLeskey
Larry E. Milan
Don and Mary Miles
Boyce and Carole Miller
Weston Milliken
Karen and Bob Mitchell
Sam and Dennis Mitchell
John and Belle
Montgomery
Lynda Moore
Marsha Moore
Peter Moore
Charles and Paula Morgan
J.F. Floyd Mortuary
John and Susan Murphy
Susan Myers
Kirk and Clare Neely
Walter and Susan Novak
Cecile and Chris Nowatka
Corry and Amy Oakes
Sandra Olson
Ned and Ansley Page
Steve and Penni Patton
Carolyn Pennell
John and Lynne Poole
Mary Potter
Harold and Liselotte
Powell
L. Perrin and Kay A Powell
Betty Price
Day Pritchartt
Philip and Frances Racine
Eileen Rampey
Karen Randall
Allison and John Ratterree
Elizabeth Refshauge
Anna S. and Charles E.
Rickell
Laura Ringo
Bertice T. Robinson
Renee Romberger
William and Carey
Rothschild
Ellen Rutter
Tony and Kimberlee
Sanchez
Gordon and Molly Sherard

Steve and Judy Sieg
Caroline and Ron Smith
Danny and Becky Smith
Donna Smith
Louis Smith
Diane Smock and Brad
Wyche
Lee and James Snell
Johanna Lewis and Richard
Spiers
Eugene and Rita Spiess
Hank and Marla Steinberg
B.G. and Sandra Stephens
Tammy and David Stokes
Laura Allen and Roger
Sullivan
Margaret Sullivan
Travis Sutton
Robert and Christine
Swager
Pat and John Tatham
Nancy Taylor
Frank Thies, III
Ray Thompson
Deno Trakas
Gloria Underwood
Diane Vecchio and John
Stockwell
Mary Helen and Gregg
Wade
Catherine Wahlen
Bill and Winnie Walsh
Lawrence and Jerri
Warren
Jennifer Washburn
Mary Ellen Wegrzyn
Cathy and Andy
Westbrook
Dave and Linda Whisnant
Karen and John B. White, Jr.
Alanna and Don Wildman
Edward S. Wildrick
William and Floride
Willard
Elizabeth "Libbo" Wise
Bob and Carolyn Wynn
Steve and Charlotte Zides
Mark Zimmerli
Suzanne and Jon Zoole

ACKNOWLEDGEMENTS

We owe a great deal of gratitude to naturalist Austin Jenkins and the many other Clemson Master Naturalist instructors who opened our eyes to the great amount of diversity throughout South Carolina. We are so thankful that the South Carolina Wildlife Federation sponsors these classes in the Midlands and provides many continuing education field trips.

A special thank you to Laurie Walden who critiqued and proofed chapters for us.

We want to thank Betsy Teter, designer Brandy Lindsey, and everyone at Hub City for their faith and hard work on this project.

HUB CITY
PRESS

Hub City Press is an independent press in Spartanburg, South Carolina, that publishes well-crafted, high-quality works by new and established authors, with an emphasis on the Southern experience. We are committed to high-caliber novels, short stories, poetry, plays, memoir, and works emphasizing regional culture and history. We are particularly interested in books with a strong sense of place. Hub City Press is an imprint of the non-profit Hub City Writers Project, founded in 1995 to foster a sense of community through the literary arts. Our metaphor of organization purposely looks backward to the nineteenth century when Spartanburg was known as the "hub city," a place where railroads converged and departed.

RECENT HUB CITY PRESS TITLES

Wedding Pulls • J.K. Daniels

Over the Plain Houses • Julia Franks

Suburban Gospel • Mark Beaver

Carolina Writers at Home • Meg Reid, editor

On Common Ground • Carroll Foster, photographer

Underground Spartanburg • Joe Mullinax, editor

Minnow • James E. McTeer II